STUDIES IN BRITISH HISTORY AND CULTURE

Volume II

Anglo-Saxons and Celts

A Study of Anti-Irish Prejudice in Victorian England

by L. P. Curtis, Jr.

UNIVERSITY OF CALIFORNIA, BERKELEY

CBS/UB

Published by the Conference on British Studies
at the University of Bridgeport, Connecticut

ACKNOWLEDGMENTS

Generous grants from the Institute of International Studies, the President's Fund for Summer Faculty Fellowships, and the Humanities Institute at Berkeley have supported the research for this essay. For the opportunity to write up some of the results of that research I am indebted to the American Council of Learned Societies and to the Warden and Fellows of Nuffield College, Oxford. This essay represents the preliminary statement or précis of what will eventually become a full length study of Anglo-Saxonism in Greater Britain and Celticism in Greater Ireland.

Many persons have provided fruitful suggestions and advice along the way to completing the present work, and to name them all would require a better memory and more space than I can command. Among the many who have helped, the following deserve particular mention: Dudley Bahlman, Reinhard Bendix, Christopher Collier, the editor of this volume, Peter Cominos, Maire Condon, Dan Davin, Joseph Donohue, Owen Dudley Edwards, David Eversley, John Kelleher, Joseph Kelly, Sheila MacArthur, J. F. A. Mason, T. W. Moody, Helen Mulvey, Raphael Samuel, and Terence de V. White.

A special note of thanks is due to those colleagues in the Department of History, Berkeley, whose encouragement, both implicit and explicit, has sustained this inquiry from the outset. The expert typing of Nora Grigsby and Kathy Goldman as well as the invaluable assistance of Jeanne Peterson deserve grateful recognition.

Produced and Distributed by New York University Press

IN MEMORIAM

M.E.C.

1930-1957

Ce lac dur oublié que hante sous le givre
Le transparent glacier des vols qui n'ont pas fui!

Mallarmé, *Plusieurs Sonnets*

Preface

Studies in British History and Culture, a joint venture of the Conference on British Studies and the University of Bridgeport, was founded in January, 1965. The first round of manuscript competition was announced at the Fall 1965 Conference meeting. No one expected then that more than forty manuscripts would be submitted in the next eighteen months.

From the screening of many readers and editors, two manuscripts have emerged as winners in the first phase of competition. John Schlight's *Monarchs & Mercenaries* and L. P. Curtis, Jr.'s *Anglo-Saxons and Celts* are the first of the series to be published. These works, which inaugurate this Monograph Series, meet many of the ideals laid down for the Series by the editors and other Conference officials who conceived it. These ideals include vigorous research, original interpretation, literary grace, and the prospect of interest among scholars in several fields. The editors were especially seeking works which would challenge traditional viewpoints.

Studies in British History and Culture generally, and these first monographs in particular, ought to be regarded as a tribute to Walter Love, the first Managing Editor, who died tragically after laying the foundation for the Series. Professor Love negotiated the production arrangement with the New York University Press, solicited and screened the initial large group of manuscripts, and handled innumerable business matters prerequisite to publishing these first books. It is our hope that *Studies in British History and Culture* will come to be regarded as a viable memorial to his energy, imagination, and devotion.

Stephen Graubard
Leland Miles
Senior Editors

CONTENTS

Anglo-Saxons
and Celts

CHAPTER I

Anglo-Saxonist Attitudes

Political historians tend to resemble the politicians they study in at least one obvious respect: they usually repeat the language of past political controversy without probing too deeply into its meaning, and, like many of their protagonists, they avoid the effort of trying to understand the wider social and cultural contexts in which events of historical significance occurred. Those phrases and slogans which were the common currency of political life in the later Victorian period such as 'integrity of empire,' 'Parnellism,' and 'Home Rule' require the kind of careful semantic scrutiny which the late Professor Koebner gave to the words 'empire' and 'imperialism'.[1] To be effective, however, the semantic approach to history must venture beyond mere definitions and come to grips with the reasons why these words were charged with certain emotions, values, and associations in the first place. As much as any aspect of modern British history, the so-called Irish Question is in need of historians who are willing to dig down beneath the surface of party manifestos and parliamentary debate in order to lay bare the realities as well as fantasies of the political conflict which made it so difficult, even impossible, for Englishmen and Irishmen to live congenially within the same cultural and political framework.

Now that the main contours of the official or administrative relations between England and Ireland have been more or less adequately drawn from the Act of Union in 1800 to the Anglo-Irish Treaty of 1921, the time has come to seek some explanations for the consistent failure of British governments, and especially the English governing classes on whom they depended for support and personnel, to cope with the Irish Question. Perhaps failure is too kind and too conventional a word. It might be more appropriate to say that generations of English politicians, civil servants, and voters managed to bring about the one thing which most of them sought to avoid in Ireland; namely the perpetuation of an intransigent party or coalition of Irish nationalists whose energies and even lives were dedicated to the creation of an executive and legislative authority in Dublin responsible to the Irish electorate and having jurisdiction over Irish affairs, however these might be defined. No matter how much importance is attached to the mistakes and injustices of English policy in Ireland before the passing of the Act of Union, the net effect of English rule in the nineteenth century was to drive hundreds of thousands of adult Irishmen and women into a camp which became increasingly hostile not just to the Imperial Parliament and executive at Westminster but to the bulk of the English people. Aided and abetted by social and economic problems in Ireland, many of which were beyond the resources of the government to eliminate or control, the Irish nationalist movement became ever more impatient for concessions, aggressive in its methods, and disenchanted with the paltry results of an agitation based on English rules of the political game. Why English policy in Ireland should have ended by bringing about the very fate which it was supposed to avoid in the form of a violent and bitter rupture between the two countries — excepting the northeast corner of Ireland — is a question that may never be answered to the satisfaction of every student of Anglo-Irish relations. But it is a question too rarely asked and one that deserves a few answers, however incomplete, even though any attempt to explain the incompatibility of England and Ireland may well end by provoking the heirs of both parties to that ancient dispute.

This essay seeks to place the formally political aspects of the Irish Question during the Victorian period within a framework composed of prevailing attitudes in England about the various races and cultures of mankind in general and about the assumed differences between Englishmen and Irishmen in particular. This framework deserves to be called both 'domestic' and 'imperial' because it is held together by a form of prejudice that transcended the conventional boundaries between political problems at home and within the Empire. The point of departure for this study has been the assumption or hypothesis that only by examining what members of the Victorian governing classes really thought about Irishmen and Irish character can one begin to understand why English policy in Ireland failed to treat the causes rather than the symptoms of Irish national aspirations. The absence herein of a detailed discussion of the actual events which affected Anglo-Irish relations during the nineteenth century does not signify a denial of the importance of political realities. But this essay does give greater emphasis to the emotional context, often camouflaged or implicitly stated, in which decisions relating to Ireland and Irish affairs were taken. As an inquiry into the role of ethnic and racial prejudice in Anglo-Irish relations, this study has more to do with wishful thinking and distortions of reality than with the reality itself. How and why a number of educated Victorians put together a crude and inflexible stereotype of Irish character or behavior out of material old and new, and the political as well as psychological significance of that stereotype constitute the main concerns of this excursion into the dimly lit world of prejudice in Victorian England.

In the present context prejudice means a prejudgment or premature assessment of someone or something based on scanty evidence and motivated by the emotional as well as social needs of the group in question.[2] The word is used here to convey that cluster of negative and patronizing attitudes and beliefs which characterized the thinking of many Englishmen and not a few Scots, Welsh, and Anglo-Irishmen about the so-called native Irish. The search for a plausible explanation of the failure of the Victorian governing classes to prevent the political rupture with Ireland which so many of them dreaded has forced the author to spend considerable time outside the pale of conventional political history. He has had to wander in less cultivated regions where the signposts are few, the people often uncommunicative, and the evidence which survives is widely scattered, elusive, and at times enigmatic. Any attempt to conduct a mining operation on the motives and thoughts of people long since dead is bound to invite some scepticism on the part of informed readers. But it is worth running a few risks in order to pursue the goal epitomized in Norman Gash's observation that the political historian's most challenging task is to seek out and identify "the implicit fundamental attitudes which condition everything but are often unconscious or taken for granted, and therefore rarely discussed and recorded."[3] Gash's perceptive remark deserves one important qualification in the context of Anglo-Irish relations. Some of the prejudices considered here were discussed frequently and openly by Victorians, even if their significance was not grasped and their motivation almost entirely obscured.

Any attempt to explain the gradual breakdown of Anglo-Irish relations in the century before World War I must sooner or later focus on the reasons why so many members of the educated and propertied classes in England opposed the demand of more than eighty percent of the Irish electorate for some form of national self-government. The most crucial question of all those that went to make up the Irish Question was whether or not the 'native Irish' could be trusted with responsibility for attending to the myriad problems of Irish government from poverty, economic stagnation, the land question, and agrarian crime to religious strife, deficiencies in the educational system, and disputes over a just contribution from Irish revenues to the Imperial Exchequer. If English politicians of the caliber of Peel and Gladstone could not manage to dispel the nightmarish quality of the Irish Question, how on earth, it was asked, could any Irishmen be found who might succeed where these two 'double first' intellects had failed? Granted that many Englishmen tended to look at Ireland and its inhabitants from a distance far greater than the mileage between London and Dublin, nevertheless those Englishmen who did pay attention to the seemingly interminable discussions of Irish affairs in Parliament, the press, and other ephemeral literature, or at dinner tables in Mayfair and Belgravia, shared in common some degree of scepticism about the capacity of the 'average' Irishman to control himself let alone manage any considerable number of his fellow countrymen. In numerous ways and on numerous occasions, relatively obscure as well as eminent Victorians gave vent to their conviction that the 'native Irish' were simply unfit to manage their affairs either on a local or national level. How else can one explain the fact that despite persistent agitation by an overwhelming majority of the Irish electorate after 1880, the Act of Union was not disturbed in its political essentials until the era of World War I; and that England, Scotland, and Wales received elective county and borough councils in 1888, whereas Ireland did not win a comparable concession, and that hedged round with heavy safeguards, until 1898? The answers to these questions are closely connected with the determination of many Englishmen to deal in terms of something called 'Irish national character' which presented a striking contrast and antithesis to the picture they had formed of their own national character. It was this image of the Irish and its symbiotic relationship with an English self-image that made it virtually impossible for educated Englishmen to "disengage the disinterested intelligence, to release it from the entanglements of party and sect," to use G. M. Young's fine phrase, and to apply that intelligence in a constructive way to the causes rather than the symptoms of estrangement and alienation between the leaders of Irish and English public opinion.[4]

Just as there was never in practice a *single* Irish Question, so there never existed a single answer to the problems which dogged English politicians and administrators in Ireland. But there was a unifying theme that ran through most of the judgments made about Ireland and the Irish in Victorian England, and that theme had a distinctly ethnic and racial character. Stated simply, this consensus amounted to an assumption or a conviction that the 'native Irish' were alien in race and inferior in culture to the Anglo-Saxons. This belief owed some of its appeal to the contrasts which had been drawn in the past between the English and the Irish by adventurers and settlers in the Tudor and Stuart periods, when the Irish countryside was being mauled and despoiled by Irish rebellion and English plantation. More to the point, however, this notion about the existence of a profound gulf between English and Irish character and culture in the nineteenth century derived a good deal of force from theories about race and national character which were steadily gaining in popularity during the Victorian period. The preference of many Englishmen for a racial explanation of Irish behavior tells us much more about the people who accepted stereotypes of Irish or Celtic behavior than it does about the actual condition of Irish society and the personalities of which it was composed. Some of the ingredients of the prevailing stereotype of Irish character contained a small but hard core of reality: it is almost impossible to measure that core with precision. Other ingredients were based on pure fancy or malice aforethought. It was not until the middle decades of the century that all the components of this stereotype were finally assembled and reproduced for a mass reading public which was by then ready to believe almost anything of a derogatory nature about the Irish people. Just how and why this caricature of 'Paddy' or the so-called Irish Celt was put together in Victorian England forms the substance of this essay.

Nowadays words like 'stereotype' and 'image' are bandied about by social historians and social scientists as though they were skeleton keys with which to unlock all the closed doors which bar the way to an understanding of human behavior. To avoid similar charges of imprecision or inflated meaning, the word 'image' is used here to convey the various associations or adjectives to which epithets like 'Paddy,' 'Celts,' or 'Gaels' gave rise in the minds of most educated Englishmen. Image connotes a theme or impression repeated endlessly with but minor variations. By the related word 'stereotype' is meant those patterns of generalized behavior which Victorians assigned to all Irishmen, women, and children whether or not they were willing to grant a few exceptions to the stereotypical rule. The word denotes here all those foibles, faults, and follies which were conjured up in English imaginations by epithets like 'Paddy' and 'Biddy.' However inconsistent some of the attributes involved in that stereotype might be, and however much the emphasis of its purveyors might shift from one trait to another in the course of the century, the essentials of what was considered to be 'Irish character' remained relatively unchanged throughout the period in question. But the prejudices which underlay and sustained that stereotype were greatly stimulated and aroused by the Home Rule agitation and the land war in Ireland during the political ascendancy of Parnell, and some of the most revealing examples of English prejudice against the Irish date from those years when the Parnellite party succeeded in transforming the cause of Irish national aspirations from a chimera into a harsh and unpleasant reality for most members of the British political elite.

The often heard argument in Victorian England about the inherent unfitness of Irishmen for self-government belongs to a pattern of thinking which I have chosen to call Anglo-Saxonism. The most important article in this creed was the notion that the Anglo-Saxon people or race, as clearly distinguished from all other races in the world, had a peculiar genius for governing themselves — and others

— by means of a constitutional and legal system that combined the highest degree of efficiency with liberty and justice. Anglo-Saxonism, as used here, represents the specifically English and Victorian form of ethnocentrism.[5] Now, as every good social scientist knows, there is more than one way to define that term, and almost all of them are inadequate. Studies of ethnocentrism conducted by psychologists and sociologists since World War II abound with different yardsticks and scales for measuring and weighing the intensity as well as the consequences of this form of prejudice. There is no need here, however, to become embroiled in the controversy which has raged around the concept of the 'authoritarian personality' and its relation to ethnocentrism.[6] For the present limited purposes, what is required is a working definition of this term like the following. Ethnocentrism characterizes that nucleus of beliefs and attitudes, cultivated and cherished by people who seek relief from some of their own anxieties and fears, which make for more or less rigid distinctions between their own group (or in-group) and some other collection of people (or out-group) with the result that the former are ranked far above the latter in the assumed hierarchy of peoples, nations, or ethnic units which together make up the species of man.[7] For the ethnocentrist all groups other than his own tend to become out-groups which are by definition inferior, subordinate, and unworthy. Ethnocentric thinking flourishes in a climate of anxiety, fear, and guilt as these emotions permeate both the individual and the class or group to which he belongs, and it is reinforced by the delusion that the values or physical proximity of the out-group somehow pose a direct threat to his own way of life. Ethnocentrism offers something of a refuge to the individual who finds the objective world — if he discovers it at all — too complex and too competitive to inhabit for any length of time and who therefore retreats into a world made up of black and white contrasts, of in-group and out-group, and of dogmatic categories about human behavior where neither qualifications nor precise measurements are to be found. Let us turn then to consider the Victorian version of ethnocentrism which bears the name of Anglo-Saxonism.

Students of nativism and ethnocentrism in America have expended far more words and energy on describing the symptoms of

Anglo-Saxonism, as they manifested themselves in the nineteenth and early twentieth centuries, than they have on explaining the phenomena in question.[8] The same cannot be said for English historians, to whom the concept of Anglo-Saxonism is unknown, foreign, or meaningless. What I mean by Anglo-Saxonism can be boiled down, with some loss of precision and flavor, to the belief that the glory of English civilization, as it had evolved over the centuries in the British Isles and then spread forth to the North American continent, the Antipodes, and beyond, was no accident or freak of nature but the result of a set of skills and talents which were the unique inheritance of a people bound together by common ancestry or blood who were conventionally known as Anglo-Saxons. The tangible successes of those who claimed this Anglo-Saxon heritage in ordering their own political, social, and economic affairs as well as those of other races, their sterling achievements in literature, the arts, and science, and their prowess in seafare and warfare provided incontrovertible proof that the so-called 'Anglo-Saxon genius' was no figment of a chauvinistic imagination. For those Englishmen who believed in the superiority of the Anglo-Saxon race and culture over all others in the world, the supreme embodiment of that genius could be found in the English Constitution which had enshrined and preserved over many centuries certain fundamental liberties, sometimes labeled Saxon, Gothic, German, Teutonic, or ancient liberties, the sum of which accounted for the moral and material progress of the modern English people. The English nation could never have overcome the many threats to its social and political stability from within as well as without, could never have risen to a position of preeminence among the great powers of the world, and could never have amassed a vast overseas empire, so the argument ran, had it not been for the innate wisdom and skills of the Anglo-Saxon race. The Victorian Anglo-Saxonist — to indulge in something of a stereotype — found his explanation for the rise of the British Empire not in Divine Providence, not in 'British luck,' and not in the universal laws of political economy, but in the distinctive racial attributes of the English people. Conversely he tried to explain the failure of other nations and people to match that achievement by the absence of those same racial traits or features.

During the middle decades of the nineteenth century most of

England's leading historians were committed to an ethnic and racial interpretation of English history, and with loving care they traced the organic growth and development of these ancient Saxon or Gothic liberties from the fifth century down to modern times. According to this Anglo-Saxonist mythology, the first seeds of what subsequently grew into the magnificent edifice of the English Constitution were planted by sturdy Saxon freemen and their racial kindred in tiny communities scattered through the great forests which lay between the Elbe and the Rhine and ranged north to the Baltic Sea. In these primitive but Arcadian communities the Saxon or German inhabitants were roughly equal and equally free, and they fought to preserve their freedom with the same tenacity and success as did their descendants who emigrated to the island of Britain in the fifth and sixth centuries. Those Saxon or German liberties which the invaders brought with them to their new island home survived such ordeals as the Norman Conquest, the Wars of the Roses, and the personal rule of both Charles I and Oliver Cromwell, and they had been given a new lease on life by the Revolutionary Settlement of 1688 and after, and by the Reform Act of 1832. Anglo-Saxonism thus assumed the existence in England of an homogeneous people or race who had possessed since time out of mind certain superior mental and physical features, and it took for granted the existence of a remarkable degree of continuity of both blood and institutions between the Jutes, Angles, and Saxons of the fifth century and the modern English people. Perhaps the most widely circulated version of this Anglo-Saxonist fairy tale was contained in the opening section of John R. Green's *A Short History of the English People*, first published in 1874:

> For the fatherland of the English race we must look far away from England itself. In the fifth century after the birth of Christ, the one country which we know to have borne the name of Angeln or the Engleland lay in the district which we now call Sleswick, a district in the heart of the peninsula which parts the Baltic from the northern seas. . . . To the north of the English in their Sleswick home lay another kindred tribe, the Jutes, whose name is still preserved in their district of Jutland. To the south of them a number of German tribes had drawn together in their

homeland between the Elbe and the Ems, and in a wide tract across the Ems to the Rhine, into the people of the Saxons. Engle, Saxon, and Jute all belonged to the same Low German branch of the Teutonic family; and at the moment when history discovers them, they were being drawn together by the ties of common blood, common speech, common social and political institutions. Each of them was destined to share in the conquest of the land in which we live; and it is from the union of all of them when its conquest was complete that the English people has sprung.[9]

So much for the geographical origins of the Anglo-Saxon peoples whose culture as well as blood represented a blend of all that was best in the Jutes, Angles, Saxons, and other German or Teutonic tribes. At the heart of that culture, once it had been carried across the North Sea to Britain virtually intact, was of course an atmosphere of freedom and a tradition of free, representative institutions. To quote Green again:

> Of the temper and life of the folk in this older England we know little. But from the glimpses which we catch of them when conquest had brought them to the shores of Britain, their political and social organization must have been that of the German race to which they belonged. The basis of their society was the free man. He alone was known as "the man", or "the churl"; and two phrases set his freedom vividly before us. He was "the free-necked man" whose long hair floated over a neck that had never bent to a lord. He was "the weaponed man", who alone bore spear and sword, for he alone possessed the right which in such a state of society formed the main check upon lawless outrage, the right of private war.[10]

Green's apotheosis of the Saxon or German freeman who carried his village liberties in a kind of holy constitutional grail from the Elbe to the Thames was a more elaborate and up-to-date statement of an idea whose roots can be traced back beyond the champions of England's ancient liberties in the Tudor-Stuart period to the discourse on *Germania* written by Tacitus.[11] Indeed, right up to the end of the nineteenth century, Anglo-Saxonist apostles were drawing on

Tacitus' description of the manners, customs, and appearance of the Germans in the hopes of providing their interpretation of early English history with some documentation, however meager that might be. This belief in the German origins of English liberties reached its fullest and most authoritative expression in the second half of the nineteenth century, that is to say, after the older faith in the forces of national character and the *volksgeist* — a faith that owed most of its inspiration to the romantic reaction against the enlightenment in Germany during the French revolution — had begun to blend with the new enthusiasm for scientific method in history, anthropology, philology, psychology, and other disciplines in the 1830's and 1840's.

A generation before Green, Sir Henry Bulwer had expressed much the same Anglo-Saxonist sentiments during a speech in the House of Commons on the protocol of the German Diet. Bulwer took advantage of the occasion to emphasize the cultural and religious as well as racial kinship of the German and English people, and he then solemnly declared: "It was in the free forests of Germany that the infant genius of our liberty was nursed. It was from the free altars of Germany that the light of our purer religion first arose. It was from one of the minor states of Germany that our Constitutional Monarchs came."[12] In the light of these and similar pious expressions about the German origins of English political and civil liberties it is possible to define Anglo-Saxonism as containing most or all of the following propositions: 1. There was an identifiable and historically authenticated race or people known as the Anglo-Saxons who shared common ties of blood, language, geographical origin, and culture and who could be traced right back to the Jutes, Angles, and Saxons who had once inhabited the region between the Baltic and the Black Forest. 2. Civil and religious liberties enjoyed no fuller expression anywhere in the world than in predominantly Anglo-Saxon societies, and this tradition of freedom was directly attributable to the peculiar genius of the Anglo-Saxons in political affairs. 3. The Anglo-Saxon peoples of the British Isles possessed a combination of virtues and talents which made them superior in all important respects to any other comparable racial or cultural group in the world. 4. Such specifically Anglo-Saxon attributes as reason, restraint, self-control, love of freedom and hatred of anarchy, respect for law and distrust of enthusiasm were actually transmissible from one generation of Anglo-

Saxons to the next in a kind of biologically determined entailed inheritance. 5. The most serious threats to the inherent superiority of the Anglo-Saxon peoples came not only from international rivalries for markets, and competition for industrial production, overseas empire, and command of the seas, but also from physiological and biological forces inside the nation or race. Among those threats were the likelihood, if not the actuality, of racial deterioration through the strains and pressures of a highly urbanized and industrialized society, or of 'race suicide' through a deliberate limitation of family size, or of the adulteration and contamination of Anglo-Saxon blood by mixture with 'foreign' blood, whether that of the Irish, Jews, Italians, French, and so on.[13]

To call Anglo-Saxonism an ideology may offend those intellectual historians who insist that the term should be applied only to bodies of ideas or principles which are coherent, systematic, and internally consistent. Anglo-Saxonism was none of these: it was above all unsystematic, illogical, unhistorical, and, at times, downright incoherent. But it had a powerful emotional appeal to Englishmen who sought some explanation for the coexistence of political stability and economic prosperity in Britain and who needed some justification for imperialist expansion in those parts of the world noted for political instability and poverty. This creed found many different apostles and preachers in the second half of the century, but historians like John Kemble, John Green, William Stubbs, Edward Freeman, Charles Kingsley, and James Anthony Froude were the most active and erudite of all those who worked to promote this faith.

Ardent Anglo-Saxonists not only regarded all Catholic Irishmen as members of an inferior race called Celts or Gaels, but they usually insisted that the Celtic people, whether in Ireland or on the Continent, had never experienced those free institutions which belonged to the Anglo-Saxon heritage. Although they may have been completely ignorant of the fact, many of those Victorians who condemned the Irish as being politically immature and suited only for despotic forms of government derived some of their Anglo-Saxonist inspiration from the 'Norman Yoke' theory of the Levellers and their radical heirs in later generations who, as Christopher Hill has shown, attacked the 'unjust' laws of their own day in the name of those ancient liberties which they imagined the Saxons had enjoyed before the Norman

Conquest.[14] There was, of course, a world of difference between the Norman Yoke school of thought, with its emphasis on popular sovereignty as against royal absolutism, and the elitist Anglo-Saxonism of the middle and late nineteenth century. That difference can best be described as one between those who made a religion out of natural rights and those who put their trust in the biological laws which governed human behavior by means of inherited racial traits. The Levellers and their radical heirs invoked the myth of a crude Saxon or Gothic democracy in England before the Conquest in order to justify their own opposition to what they regarded as monarchial or aristocratic tyranny, whereas the Victorian Anglo-Saxonists relied on much the same kind of myth, by now weighted down with the latest scientific discoveries of anthropologists and ethnologists in order to preserve the *status quo* at home and advance the cause of empire abroad. The authoritarian and paternalistic note in Anglo-Saxonism stands out as prominently as did the libertarian and commonwealth strain in the older Norman Yoke theory.

The emotions that endowed Anglo-Saxonism with such wide appeal in England cut right across conventional party boundaries and social classes. They could be found among Whigs as well as Radicals, Liberals as well as Conservatives. And in the enormous body of literature, both ephemeral and more permanent, which the Victorians bequeathed to posterity, it is not difficult to discover references to Irish unfitness for self-government, Irish incompetence in business and domestic economy, Irish deficiency in intellectual power, and Irish obtuseness in scientific matters. Allusions to the proverbial Irish faults of violence, indolence, and intemperance are strewn through novels, pamphlet literature, works of history, and cartoons or prints. Where these ethnocentric assumptions came from and why they had such a widespread appeal among the Victorian governing classes are questions that have a direct bearing on the reasons why Ireland was, to quote G. M. Young again, "the one irreparable disaster" of English history.

One cannot begin to understand the reasons for that failure unless one is prepared to accept the hypothesis that the Irish Question was in all but a physical sense essentially an English question. That is to say, the Irish Question, as seen in England, was what a number of Englishmen thought and perhaps wanted it to be. Most members of the governing classes saw Irish questions and the Irish people through Anglo-Saxonist glasses, and those glasses were so ground and tinted as to impose a particular form and color on all things Celtic or Hibernian. What they saw through their lenses had a great deal to do with their need to create a hard and fast category for so-called Irish national character and relatively little to do with the social, political, economic, and psychological realities of millions of Irishmen, women, and children.

Although this study is concerned primarily with Anglo-Saxonist attitudes about Celtic Ireland, it must not be assumed that all educated Englishmen succumbed to this cluster of ethnocentric prejudices or that the much abused Irish people stood silently by while English presses churned out stereotypes of life in 'Paddy-land.' In England the thrust of Anglo-Saxonist prejudices against the Celtic Irish and other inferior races of the world set up a countercurrent in the 1880's and 1890's which may be called environmentalism. Those who subscribed to an environmentalist interpretation of human behavior could claim that they were the heirs of the enlightenment belief that human societies were regulated or governed by universal laws which determined the conditions, physical, social, and political, in which men lived. Environmentalists were basically optimistic about human nature, and like Helvetius and Beccaria they believed that good laws made good men. They had little or no time for a concept so vague, insidious, and pessimistic as race, and they scorned the notion that national character was a permanent, immutable, and inherited force which could never be altered by the hand of man. Entirely opposed to the Anglo-Saxonist emphasis upon the transmission of desirable or undesirable traits through the bloodstream from one generation to another within the same racial unit, the environmentalists, as will be noted later, found their key to human behavior in the total historical and contemporary context of any given country or nation.

In Ireland the Anglo-Saxonist mythology also set up a countercurrent or cultural resistance movement. Some Irishmen replied to their detractors in England with oaths against the bloody, base Sassenach or treacherous Saxon. But after the 1830's there appeared an ever more sophisticated rebuttal in the form of a Celticist mythology which culminated in the Irish literary revival or renaissance during the last few decades before 1914. Drawing upon many different talents and disciplines, Celticism tried to accomplish for the 'Irish race' what Anglo-Saxonism had managed to do for the 'English race,' namely to raise the people concerned to an exalted position of cultural and racial superiority far above the nearest claimants to that title. According to the theories of Celticist scholars and publicists in the last third of the century, the modern Irish were the direct descendants of a pure and holy race, composed of Firbolgs, Tuatha de Dananns, and Milesians, whose ancient institutions, veneration for learning, and religious zeal made Saxon culture during the two or three centuries before the Norman Conquest look nothing less than barbarian. The subject of Celticism deserves much more attention than is possible here, but in chapter nine the reader will find a few clues about the ways in which ethnocentric Irish men and women sought to combat heavy doses of Anglo-Saxonist venom with a Celticist serum of their own making.

To sum up then, the study of Anglo-Saxonist attitudes about Ireland and the Irish brings into focus a pattern of sharply delineated contrasts between assumed stereotypes of Irish and English — or Celtic and Anglo-Saxon — behavior. These contrasts were sustained by ethnic prejudices which increased in English minds the already wide gap between the social and economic development of the two countries. The effect of these prejudices was to reduce the Irish Question, especially after the mid-century, to an apparent conflict between two fundamentally incompatible races. An all-encompassing dichotomy between Anglo-Saxons and Irish Celts was the construction which many Victorians both in England and Ireland placed upon Anglo-Irish relations in that period. For most upper and middle class Englishmen the so-called Celtic fringe was more than a geographical expression, the butt of many jokes, and the favorite hunting ground of grouse-shooters and Liberal electoral agents; it was a distinct ethnic and cultural reality, a barren and semi-civilized region in the west populated with various Celtic tribes entirely out of step with the enterprising and civilized Anglo-Saxon south and east. The antithesis of Anglo-Saxon and Celt took on an ever more racialist hue as scientistic theories about race and racial traits gained greater currency among the later Victorians. The Irish Question was both a symptom and a contributing cause of race consciousness in England,

and as such the historian must constantly bear in mind the differences between the realities of Irish life and the appearances they assumed in the minds of Anglo-Saxonists in England and America.

Like all forms of ethnocentric thinking Anglo-Saxonism came in assorted sizes and degrees of intensity, and the militancy of the creed depended upon such variables as personality structure, social and economic position, education, political persuasion, and religious conviction. The meaning of Anglo-Saxonism is lost, however, if one persists in thinking that formal party boundaries such as those between Liberals and Conservatives coincided with those barriers which divided militant Anglo-Saxonists from non-Anglo-Saxonists or environmentalists. Anglo-Saxonism was not confined to any one party, class, or occupational group or region. It permeated the thinking of Radicals like Dilke and Chamberlain and Liberals like Freeman and Green, but it found an even more congenial home among Tories like Froude, Stubbs, and Lord Salisbury. Indeed, the best examples of Anglo-Saxonist prejudice against the Irish Celts emanate from the Unionist coalition which was hastily patched together in the winter of 1886 in order to destroy the first Home Rule Bill. The many dire predictions made by Unionists about the disastrous effects Home Rule would have upon Ireland and the empire owed much of their inspiration to this ethnocentrism, and throughout the debates on the question of Home Rule the underlying assumption of almost all those who opposed Gladstone's two bills was that Irish Celts were in no way suited for such luxuries as Anglo-Saxon liberties and institutions.

CHAPTER II

The Varieties of Anti-Irish Prejudice

If Anglo-Saxonism provided the main cultural context in which the Irish Question was discussed and treated in England, especially during the period of the Home Rule agitation led by Parnell, it should not be assumed that the derogatory stereotype of the Irish Celt which many Victorians carried with them was a brand-new invention of the 1850's or 1860's. Some of the ingredients of that stereotype were as old as the first violent contacts between the Anglo-Norman invaders and the indigenous people of Ireland. In the 1180's, for example, Giraldus Cambrensis, that jaundiced and impetuous observer of the Welsh and the Irish, provided King Henry II with the following picture of the inhabitants of Ireland:

> Gens igitur haec gens barbara, et vere barbara. Quia non tantum barbaro vestium ritu, verum etiam comis et barbis luxuriantibus, juxta modernas novitates, incultissima; et omnes eorum mores barbarissimi sunt.[1]

Equally unflattering images of the Irish date from the later decades of the sixteenth century when Englishmen like Barnaby Rich, Richard Stanyhurst, William Good, Fynes Moryson, and Edmund Spenser recorded their thoughts and impressions of the gulf between the 'wild Irishry' and civilized Englishmen like themselves.[2] Ever since the first English (or Anglo-Norman, Anglo-Scottish, and Anglo-Welsh) efforts to colonize parts of Ireland beyond the Pale, and especially during the long, painful cycle of settlement, rebellion, war, confiscation, plantation, and renewed rebellion in the Tudor-Stuart period, there

17

had been an increasing tendency on the part of Englishmen to differentiate in theory as well as law between native Irish and English patterns of behavior. This tendency was underlined by the widespread
conviction that Englishmen who stayed too long in Ireland were
bound to go to seed or be corrupted and dragged down to the primitive, if not barbaric, culture of the 'mere Irishry.' Observers like Barnaby Rich and Fynes Moryson made few allowances for the more
brutal aspects of Irish life because their frame of reference was so
much more that of urban and aristocratic than of rural and plebeian
England. Having little or no awareness of the unsettling effects which
the forceful and armed English presence had upon Irish society, they
jumped to the conclusion that the Irish people were a turbulent, semi-
nomadic, treacherous, idle, dirty, and belligerent lot who reminded
them of the 'savages' or Indians of North America.[3] The continuities
of English thinking about the so-called native Irish, from the time of
the Henrician reformation to Catholic emancipation, far outweigh the
discontinuities. For centuries self-consciously civilized Englishmen
had taken for granted their innate superiority over the Irish in every
category and respect which went to make up 'civilization.' Doubtless
some of this assumed superiority derived from the undeniable fact
that the English — to use that hybrid term — did indeed occupy parts
of Ireland and did eventually succeed in establishing by force and by
threat of force some semblance of monarchial authority in the country. So persistent has been this theme of English cultural and racial
superiority over the Irish that one begins to suspect the existence
among those who tried to subdue and rule the Irish of a deep-seated
need to justify their confiscatory and homicidal habits in that country.

What some Englishmen described as a process of Anglicization
in Ireland amounted in practice to a policy of enforced acculturation
with the object of converting the 'Irishry' into docile hewers of wood
and efficient drawers of water for the old and new English settlers.
The goal of Mountjoy and other Lord Deputies was not just to suppress Irish rebellions, but to make the native Irish conform as much
as possible to the English working classes in respect of manners, dress,
religion, and, above all, obedience to English law; and the penalties
for nonconformity usually ranged from expropriation to extermina-
tion.

If there was indeed a new element in English attitudes towards the Irish in the Victorian era, it was bound up with the idea of race or with that amalgam of ostensibly scientific doctrines, subjective data, and ethnocentric prejudices which was steadily gaining respectability among educated men in Western Europe during the first half of the century. In England the idea of race as *the* determinant of human history and human behavior held an unassailable position in the minds of most Anglo-Saxonists, but at no time, not even when Fenian explosions or the assassination of Lord Frederick Cavendish in 1882 shocked the English public, were Anglo-Saxonist prejudices confined exclusively to the question of race. The Catholic, working class Irish were also the victims of prejudice based upon religious and social class differences.

In the prolonged debate during the Victorian period about the proper way to deal with the Irish Question there were three leitmotivs which appeared again and again in varying combinations and proportions in parliament, cabinet councils, newspapers, and on the hustings. These leitmotivs represented three kinds of prejudice based on race, class, and religious differences, and together they made up the most active ingredients of Anglo-Saxonism as it affected or impinged upon the Irish Question. These themes may be loosely translated into the negative statement that the real trouble with the Irish was that they were not Anglo-Saxon, upper class, or Protestant. There are obvious limitations to such a categorization, chief among them being the assumption that any of these types of prejudice can be neatly extricated from the closely woven fabric of Anglo-Saxonism. But it is the constant recurrence of these themes in Victorian society which goes some way to justify an attempt to dissect a corporate prejudice.[4]

To begin with the more modern of these prejudices, the word race always seems to cry out for definition, if only because those who use it so rarely bother to explain their meaning. The word was a far more effective explanation of human affairs when left undefined and unqualified. But one *caveat* is in order. Throughout the nineteenth century Englishmen continued to use the word in a more neutral and traditional sense to designate a particular class or category such as a 'race of kings' or a 'race of yeomen.' This highly ambiguous word must therefore be taken in context, lest the false impression be spread that every Englishman who talked or wrote about 'race' was a racist in the same class as Gobineau, H. S. Chamberlain, or Madison Grant. The word was indeed used in an ever more biological and physiological sense after the 1830's, and Anglo-Saxonists usually applied it to any identifiable ethnic unit or group of people possessing a set of apparently unique physical as well as mental characteristics. To most educated Victorians, race, as interpreted in its newer and more scientistic sense, connoted the more or less lasting divisions of mankind into groups of men and women who could claim descent from a common ancestor and who therefore shared the same blood and traits associated with that physiological heritage. After the mid-century, more and more self-styled experts in the science of man saw in race that force or agency which had shaped the destiny of mankind, which accounted for the rise and fall of civilizations, and which dictated almost all forms of change and continuity in human societies. In the 1840's and after, many anthropologists and ethnologists used the word in this sweeping and apocalyptic sense, and educated laymen were not slow to absorb this 'scientific' interpretation and to treat race as the key to understanding not only the past and the present but also the future.[5]

If Ashley Montagu is correct in his assertion that 'race' is "man's most dangerous myth" — and for that reason ought to be eliminated from the language — the reason lies partly in the fact that it served so many of its users as something akin to a lightning conductor through which many emotions could be effectively discharged.[6] For most Anglo-Saxonists the word was a catchall concept into which many different and conflicting feelings were poured without any attempt to analyze them. Rarely defined, the word served a number of purposes in both lay and scientific circles, and in the second half of the century it came into increasing use as an instrument for relegating millions of people, who belonged, of course, to out-groups, to everlasting inferiority on the strength of what looked like overwhelming scientific evidence. As the novels, memoirs, and genealogical 'studbooks' of the Victorians amply attest, many Englishmen were obsessed with the notion that genius, eccentricity, or other mental traits were the product of hereditary transmission through the bloodstream from one generation to the next, and the surest way to perpetuate those characteristics was to marry within the same race or stock. These notions of racial inheritance were supported by the findings of biologists, anthropologists, and doctors like Robert Knox and James Cowles Prichard. Middle and upper class Victorians may not have lived by concepts of blood and racial lineage alone, but they certainly spent an inordinate amount of time worrying about their own pedigrees or blood stock as well as those of their sons-in-law and daughters-in-law; and the assumptions they made about the importance of these hereditary features had more than a slight bearing on their ideas about the right and the wrong way to govern their own working classes as well as the non-Anglo-Saxon races of the world.

In the mid-nineteenth century most educated Englishmen were brought up to believe that there were at least five distinct races or ethnic groups represented by the modern population of the British Isles. These races were usually labelled Britons (the aboriginal inhabitants of Britain, some of whom were called Belgae and Picts), Saxons (often subdivided into Jutes, Angles, Saxons, Frisians, Goths, Germans, and so on), Celts (usually subdivided into the Cymry or Cimbri of Wales, the Gaels of Western Scotland, and the Celts or Gaels of Ireland), Danes (who belonged to the Scandinavian, Norse, or Viking race), and the Normans (who were sometimes regarded as Norsemen in French or Gallic clothing). Now there was constant disputation among the experts as to whether or not the Britons were really Celts, whether the Celts were blonde or dark, tall or short, whether the Saxons had wiped out the Britons or had mixed their blood with them, whether the Celtic tribes of Ireland had come directly from the Continent or had passed through England and Wales on the way, whether the Normans were more racially akin to the Saxons than to the Danes, and so on.[7] But the point is that many Victorians not only accepted this five-fold racial division of the modern British people but actually assigned quite distinct traits or patterns of behavior to each of these groups. These racial and ethnic distinctions sustained the 'sword and buckler' historical novels of Sir Walter Scott, Lord Lytton, Charles Kingsley, and their imitators, just as they pervaded the discussion of the English governing classes about their relations with the Irish, the Scots, and the Welsh.

The very absence of any objective methods of determining the exact proportion of so-called Saxon, Norman, or Celtic blood in their ancestry made these beliefs all the more plausible to Victorians. Indeed they had no factual basis for their notions about the remote origins of these 'races' and therefore lacked any way of knowing the degree of racial purity or integrity which they had originally represented. Needless to say the associations which Anglo-Saxonists made between race, blood, culture, and nation on the one hand and the political, social, and emotional behavior of any people on the other were not based on logical argument or convincing data, and like all simple generalizations about racial and national character they emanated from a compulsion to divide mankind into watertight or rather blood-tight categories on the basis of subjectively perceived physical and mental characteristics. On such a flimsy foundation Anglo-Saxonists based their stereotype of Irish Celtic behavior.

When Anglo-Saxonists referred to the Irish race or to Irish Celts, they usually meant by these phrases all Irish-born persons along with their relatives and descendants in other lands who were neither Protestants living in Ulster nor Protestant landlords living in some other province of Ireland. The vast majority of Irishmen were thus considered to be Celtic as well as Catholic, these two categories being taken as almost but not quite interdependent. Those Englishmen who insisted that the Irish belonged to a distinctly different or alien race took it for granted that they possessed a set of permanent traits which marked them off from all the non-Celtic peoples or races of the world. The Irishman, to use an expression that Conor Cruise O'Brien has called the "pejorative singular," was assumed by Anglo-Saxonists to have a character composed of those traits or attributes which were most deprecated in respectable English society. Like the leopard, the Celt was incapable of changing his spots, save through many generations of intermarriage with some other race. While all Anglo-Saxonists believed that the Catholic Irish were a branch of the extensive Celtic race, and some of them insisted that the Irish were the most 'Celtic' of all the Celts, Unionists were at pains after 1886 to assert that the fact of Irish racial solidarity did not mean that they constituted a nation. Any admission on their part that the boundaries of race and nationhood or nationality coincided would, of course, have gone far to legitimize the Irish nationalist demand for Home Rule, and that would have been unthinkable for all but a few Anglo-Saxonists.[8]

The study of ethnic and racial prejudice in the past presents the historian with a number of problems, some of them insuperable owing to the fact that the intolerant personalities in question belong to people long since dead. Men and women can be and often are guarded about some of their prejudices. They may wish to conceal them from certain audiences including posterity for political, social, or personal reasons, and they may prefer to save their candid opinions for the privacy of their homes or the sanctity of their clubs. Fortunately there were some Victorians who were not as reticent about revealing their anti-Irish and other prejudices as they might have been, and on the basis of the evidence they have left behind it is possible to argue that the assumed differences between Anglo-Saxons and Celts were as real to them as were those two luxury liners, the S. S. *Teutonic* and the S. S. *Celtic,* which carried many prominent Englishmen and Irishmen across the Atlantic in the 1880's. The other major difficulty confronting the student of prejudice in the past concerns the residue of reality in the stereotype which flourished at any given time and place. The question is not whether there were *some* Irishmen in the nineteenth century who were idle, dissolute, violent, intemperate, dirty, garrulous, and emotionally unstable, because of course there were some who answered this description. The important questions are how many Irishmen actually did fit the stereotype, by what methods or criteria were the mental traits of Irishmen evaluated, and how many Englishmen, Frenchmen, Germans, or Americans fell into the same category. For these questions there are unfortunately no answers readily available.

It is not hard to find evidence in Victorian England of the sharp distinction which Englishmen drew between Anglo-Saxons and Celts. It is, however, much more difficult to know or guess accurately just which people were included in such groups as Anglo-Saxons, Teutons, Goths, or Aryans and Celts, Gaels, Cymri, Milesians, Picts, or Celto-Iberians. In order to discover some of the attributes which Victorians assigned to these ethnic divisions the historian must examine many kinds of material ranging from parliamentary debates to poems, novels, jokes, and cartoons. Anecdotal anthologies and dictionaries of slang and racial slurs (also known as ethnophaulisms) provide much valuable information for the student of past prejudice.[9] For reasons of space the discussion of anti-Irish prejudice or anti-Celticism will be confined mostly to anthropologists, historians, publicists, and members of the British 'political nation' who expressed their opinions about the Irish and their character. But it should be remembered that the examples of anti-Celticism mentioned below represent only a fraction of the prejudices which found their way to the surface of Victorian culture and society.

There was, of course, something more than ethnic and racial prejudice at work in the minds of those Victorians who had to decide on the best course to follow in Irish affairs. Sensitivity to class distinctions and a habit of looking down on the Irish peasantry as peasants and not just as Celts also played a role in the denial of Home Rule and other concessions to the Irish people. As Philip Mason has suggested in his psychological interpretation of the British colonial experience, *Prospero's Magic*, the interaction of race and class prejudice went far to color the thinking of the English governing classes toward their colonial subjects. For some upper class Englishmen, the English working classes were almost a race apart, having darker skin and hair than their social superiors, and having more traits in common with their Celtic counterparts in Ireland than with the supposedly Norman aristocracy at home.[10] Race prejudice alone cannot account for the strength of English resistance to the demands of Parnell and his party in 1886 and afterwards. Anglo-Saxonists tended to harbor strong class prejudices, and there was nothing unusual about this situation because race prejudice has almost always been associated with resentments and fears arising out of distinctions of class or caste.[11] The lowly social and occupational status of the mass of Irish immigrants in Britain served to enhance their reputation of inferiority among respectable Englishmen, and at the same time that status presented an economic and social threat to those classes in England who stood to lose work or status or both to Irish competition for unskilled labor. The intimate relationship between class and race consciousness is borne out by the fact that the word race was also used throughout the century as a synonym for class. The "double dose of original sin" with which some Englishmen discredited the Irish referred as much to their inferior social position as to their racial and cultural inferiority.

It is not easy in practice to distinguish between those prejudices founded on race and those on class consciousness; they overlapped one another and in their constant interaction they became fused and confused. Not only were the Irish in Britain looked down upon as

being socially inferior by almost all Englishmen except the lowest of
the working classes, but there is some reason to believe that this sense
of superiority on the part of the English gradually increased in
the course of the nineteenth century as the Catholic emancipation
crisis excited militant Protestantism, as O'Connell's repeal agitation
alarmed defenders of the *status quo*, and as a more extreme form of
Irish nationalism in the late 1870's and 1880's forced Liberals and
Conservatives alike to fear for the security of the Act of Union
and the integrity of the empire. The more militant nationalist movement which grew out of Parnell's negotiations with ex-Fenians and
Irish-American leaders in 1878-79 tended to aggravate the class prejudice of Anglo-Saxonists against the Irish because the newer Parnellite members of Parliament in the 1880's were doubly damned for
being in Parliament in the first place and for not being gentlemen in
the tradition of Grattan and Flood.[12] Many middle and upper class
Englishmen found it impossible to separate their hostility to the immoderate nationalism — some called it republicanism, socialism, and
anarchy — of the Parnellite 'New Departure' from their profound
distaste at seeing Irish M.P.'s, who were not considered gentlemen by
any stretch of the Liberal imagination, make havoc of the procedural
rules in the Commons. Few, if any, of the Irish nationalist members
elected in 1885 were regarded by English politicians and their sup-
porters as men of birth, breeding, or education, and there was increasing resentment at the apparent fact that the Irish section of the House
was filling up with shopkeepers, farmers, journalists, and provincial
country solicitors who lacked political as well as social manners.[13] To
Anglo-Saxonists who liked to fit all Irish nationalists into their stereotype, Parnell was an exasperating exception because he was both a
gentleman landowner and a man with very little 'Irish blood' in his
veins. Class prejudice aimed at those Parnellite members who were
not large landowners or prominent Dublin barristers was indeed in-
timately related to English resentment at the politics and obstruction-
ist methods espoused by these men, and these prejudices also helped
to polarize the British 'political nation' over the Irish question in the
1880's.

The conflation of race and class prejudice in Anglo-Saxonist
minds, and its convergence on the issue of Home Rule in the 1880's,
did not preclude a third form of prejudice, namely religious bigotry

against the Roman Catholic Church in general and against Irish Catholics in particular. In Victorian England the words Irish and Catholic were usually inseparable, and few Irish Catholics were allowed to forget that English Protestants regarded their religious beliefs as a mixture of anathema, superstition, and papal despotism. Excepting the upper strata of Irish society, the social gulf between Protestant and Catholic in Ireland was virtually tangible. Granted the presence of a few Protestants in Parnell's party, apart from the leader himself, granted the fact that Protestants and Catholics worked together in the ranks of the Royal Irish Constabulary and in government offices in Dublin, nevertheless Irish nationalism was often seen by both Englishmen and Anglo-Irishmen as a movement kept alive in the countryside by parish priests and the more irreconcilable bishops like Doctors Croke and Walsh. The battle cry of Ulster Unionists in the early 1890's, "Home Rule means Rome Rule," appealed to many Protestants in England; and the anti-clerical content of Unionist propaganda reached formidable proportions during the second Home Rule Bill agitation in the early 1890's. Religious conflict in Ireland could claim a long and bloody pedigree, and even after the victory of Catholic emancipation had been consolidated, the fact of religious rivalry laid a heavy and discriminating hand on almost every facet of Irish society and political life. It would be hard then to exaggerate the importance of Protestant prejudice, tinged with an Orange hue, to the Anglo-Saxonist image of Ireland and the Irish.

In some respects the nature of anti-Irish prejudice among the English governing classes underwent no substantial change in its component parts from one end of the nineteenth century to the other. A few examples taken from *Hansard* may serve to illustrate this point. In February, 1811, Mr. Fuller, the member for Surrey, treated the House of Commons to a fine display of Protestant fervor, when he exclaimed: "I have no great faith in Catholic emancipation. I think that there is a radical and rooted antipathy between England and Ireland. Well, then, try Catholic emancipation, if you think it will do. I care no more for a Catholic than I do for a Chinese."[14] Some twenty-five years later Lord Lyndhurst protested against municipal reform in Ireland on the ground that the Irish were an "alien people" who spoke a different language and professed a different religion.[15] And in April, 1893, Sir Ellis Ashmead Bartlett, the colorful Unionist who had been born in Brooklyn, opposed the second Home Rule Bill because it meant "placing the best part of . . . [Ireland] under the control of the worst, the loyal under the disloyal, the honest under the dishonest, and the peaceful and the industrious under the idle and thriftless."[16]

There are, in fact, so many indications of the continuity of anti-Irish sentiment in Victorian England that clear-cut stages or benchmarks in this pattern of ethnocentric thinking do not stand out as boldly as do the political landmarks in Anglo-Irish relations. One might almost say that anti-Irish prejudices constitute one of the longest secular trends in English cultural history. The evidence accumulated for this study suggests, however, that Anglo-Saxonist propaganda and mythology reached something of a peak or high plateau between the 1860's and the early 1890's, although there are some striking examples of these attitudes just before and just after this period. If Unionist politicians continued to indulge in dogmatic stereotypes of Irish character in the course of their bitter resistance to Home Rule after 1893, the degree of Anglo-Saxonism in the writings of anthropologists and historians fell off in the last decade of the century. This gradual decline may be explained not only by the deaths of the older, more blatant Anglo-Saxonists among them but also by the advent of somewhat more objective methods and more thoroughly documented studies of early Irish history and ethnology.

Such, in any event, were the general trends in the pattern of Anglo-Saxonist attitudes. The various smaller and subtler shifts in emphasis on the subject of Irish behavior within the Victorian era usually depended on such variables as the intensity of political agitation and agrarian crime in Ireland, the presence or absence of charismatic leaders like O'Connell, Davitt, and Parnell, and the rate of Irish emigration into English villages, towns, and cities. These minor changes in public opinion also depended to some extent on the existence of other issues in Great Britain of sufficient local or national importance to divert attention from Irishmen and Irish affairs. Indeed, there were Englishmen in the nineteenth century — perhaps more than most historians have reckoned — for whom there was no such thing as the Irish Question but instead a personal reaction of irritation, resentment, or hostility to those Irish whom they saw or read about in their newspapers, who lived in the slums of their cities and towns, and who built their railways, laid their bricks, washed their dishes, frequented their pubs, and filled their jails.

As we will see in Chapter Seven, much the same pattern of Anglo-Saxonist thinking appeared almost simultaneously among the same or analogous classes in American cities and universities, especially those on the eastern seaboard. Anglo-Saxonism was by no means a phenomenon confined to the British Isles. It appeared in slightly different guises in North America and in other parts of the world where men claiming an Anglo-Saxon heritage and some respectability by the standards of their 'new' societies were gathered together into communities and in Orange Lodges which felt threatened by the intrusion of Irish Celtic and other 'alien' peoples who did not or who would not conform to Anglo-Saxonist criteria of civilization. The transatlantic and transpacific dimensions of Anglo-Saxonism, and the ways in which they impinged on anti-Irish prejudices in those places where Irish immigration, especially after the great famine, was most concentrated, deserve closer attention than can be provided here.

In so far as it can be identified and isolated from the religious and class components of Anglo-Saxonist attitudes, the role of race or ethnic prejudice in the English image of Ireland during the Victorian years constitutes the central strand in this essay. Such a selective approach may be justified by the fact that in the second half of the nineteenth century racial explanations of human behavior, indeed of all human history, gained greater acceptance in educated circles in England and on the Continent than ever before. Although distortions of Darwinian concepts of competition and evolution through natural selection did indeed promote sensational theories about the deadly struggle among the races of man for survival and supremacy, the *Origin of Species* itself should not be regarded as a cause of the kind of thinking which relegated Irish Celts and other so-called races to a position of inherent inferiority vis-à-vis the Anglo-Saxons in the assumed hierarchy of mankind. It is true that both in England and America social Darwinists popularized the notion that what Darwin had written about "the preservation of favoured races in the struggle for life" applied with greater force to human beings than to the pigeons he actually had in mind.[17] But the scientific antecedents of this race thinking date back far beyond the year 1859, and Darwin himself cannot be credited with responsibility for the relatively sudden and spontaneous burst of scientific enthusiasm in the 1840's which led to the founding of Ethnological Societies in most of the capitals of Western Europe as well as in New York. Launched by keen students of human behavior who called themselves ethnographers, ethnologists, and anthropologists, these societies served to crystallize many of the current theories about race and racial characteristics. Their members kept in touch with one another through the media of professional journals and conferences as well as through private channels.[18] Some of them were so confident about their ability to discern those laws of human behavior which governed the rise and fall of civilizations that they hoped to serve as advisors to the statesmen and administrators who were responsible for making decisions affecting the 'growth' or 'decay' of their countries.

Members of the London Ethnological Society had not pursued their investigations into the origins, varieties, and behavior of primitive as well as civilized man for many years before clashes of personality and differences of opinion over the methods and substance of their discipline produced serious rifts in their ranks. In a burst of renewed enthusiasm as well as controversy in the 1860's Anthropological Societies were founded in most of the same European cities. Not for another decade was the rivalry between the Ethnological and Anthropological societies of London sufficiently resolved to permit the amalgamation of the two.[19] Most of the English ethnologists of the 1850's and 1860's came from middle and upper middle class families, and their professions included medicine, law, journalism, and the church. Archaeologists, army officers, geographers, professional explorers, not to mention gentlemen of leisure, could also be found in their ranks. In the rapidly burgeoning field of anthropology some of them stumbled about like the untrained amateurs they were. Few, if any, could lay claim to the versatility and intellectual stature of James Cowles Prichard, who made his mark in philology, medical psychology, and ethnology while keeping up a busy medical practice throughout his career; and none of them could match the acumen and learning of E. B. Tylor or Sir Henry Maine. For most, fortunately not all, of this new generation of anthropologists the word race had acquired the status of a universally applicable doctrine that could be used to uncover those aspects of human behavior which had long puzzled their predecessors.

Among the leading apostles of race consciousness in England was Benjamin Disraeli, whose views on race, as expressed in his novels, came close in some respects to those favored by his Anglo-Saxonist contemporaries. Disraeli espoused the deterministic meaning of race because he wished to establish the fact that the Jews were a supremely gifted people who were head and shoulders above the other races of the world in all important cultural respects. Sidonia, that all-wise and mysterious millionaire who makes such dramatic appearances in *Coningsby* and *Tancred,* personified Disraeli's own fantasies about the genius of the Jewish race. Among Sidonia's many declarations on the importance of race and racial purity, the following passage from *Tancred* must have gratified many an Anglo-Saxonist.

> But England flourishes. Is it what you call civilisation that makes England flourish? Is it the universal development of the faculties of man that has rendered an island, almost unknown to the ancients, the arbiter of the world? Clearly not. It is her inhabitants that have done this; it is an affair of race. A Saxon race, protected by an insular position, has stamped its diligent and methodic character on the century. And when a superior race, with a superior idea to Work and Order, advances, its state will be progressive, and we shall, perhaps, follow the example of the desolate countries. All is race; there is no other truth.[20]

Half a century later Houston Stewart Chamberlain had occasion to borrow some of the last sentence in order to document his own extravagant theories about racial determinism.

By the 1860's the idea of race as the determinant of both individual and collective behavior was firmly implanted in the minds of an influential minority of men in the British Isles most of whom read and, in some cases, contributed articles to such periodicals as the *Quarterly Review,* the *Nineteenth Century,* the *Fortnightly Review,* and the various anthropological and ethnological reviews which began publication after the mid-century. The certitude with which many of these men used the concept of race to establish the superiority of the Anglo-Saxon people was matched only by the strength of their conviction that this racial and cultural preeminence was menaced in a number of ways by other races and nations as well as classes. Whether or not these race conscious scientists of society subscribed to monogenist, polygenist, or Darwinian explanations of the origins of the races of man, the fact is that a number of them accepted in part or in its entirety Lyell's theory, later taken up by Darwin, about the inheritance of acquired characteristics. Some of these anthropologists went further and insisted that human behavior as well as physical features were molded by the law of the hereditary transmission of racial characteristics. In other words, those attributes which distinguished Englishmen from Irishmen were more or less unalterable and would be passed on, ostensibly through special cells in the bloodstream, from one generation of Anglo-Saxons or Celts to the next.[21] Only miscegenation or hybridization of the two races, it was argued, could alter, over a long period of time, those racial distinctions which were obvious even to laymen.

The period of most intense Anglo-Saxonism in England, which runs from the 1860's to the early 1890's, represented the apogee of British power and influence in the world. The commercial, financial, agricultural, and industrial prosperity of the third quarter of the century; the confidence of Englishmen in their political stability, in spite of a fair degree of ministerial instability; the tangible fact of expanding formal and informal empire overseas, and the conviction that the *Pax Britannica* really did serve the best interests of the rest of the world all tended to reinforce ethnocentric assumptions about the genius of the Anglo-Saxon people for ordering their lives and those of other people with a maximum of justice, liberty, and efficiency. In order to complete this flattering self-image it was necessary only to attribute the moral and material achievements of the English people and their kindred around the world to those free Saxon or German institutions which had first seen the light of day in the woods and forests of Schleswig and those German districts lying between the Elbe and the Rhine. It was those embryonic liberties which the sturdy Hengest and Horsa had carried ashore after beaching their boat on the Isle of Thanet in the middle of the fifth century. And it was this myth which some leading English historians were prepared to accept and perpetuate in the third quarter of the nineteenth century.

Those Victorians who basked in the emotional luxury of Anglo-

Saxonism drew some of their inspiration and many of their precedents from the so-called English Gothicists of the seventeenth and eighteenth centuries who had held that the ancient laws and institutions of England, above all Parliament, were not only German or Gothic in origin but had served for centuries to protect the liberties of Saxon freemen against the acts of tyrannical kings and chieftains. The fullest expression of this legend about England's Gothic constitution may be traced back to the constitutional conflicts of the early Stuart period, although its roots lie much deeper in the past. In the second half of the seventeenth century, as Samuel Kliger has shown, a group of resourceful parliamentarians elaborated this Gothic tale in order to justify their opposition to the exercise of the royal prerogative.[22] In the hands of men like Sir William Temple, Robert Molesworth, Thomas Blount, Sir William Penn, and other worthies, the idea of England's German liberties became as respectable and sacrosanct to the Gothicists as the idea of the ancient constitution and the fundamental law had been to the jurists and lawyers of an earlier generation.[23] Selecting the evidence they needed in the form of the 'folk-motes' or councils of the ancient Goths and Saxons, the Gothicists not only compiled a pseudohistorical case against Stuart 'depotism' but helped to refurbish the prevalent image of the Goths which had made them seem a rude and barbarous people.[24]

In the nineteenth century the word Gothic was applied more often to forms of architecture, art, and fiction than to an ethnic unit or race, and what had once been labelled Gothic liberties now became Anglo-Saxon, English, or occasionally German. If the labels changed from time to time, the main message stayed intact: only the Saxons and their English descendants knew how to live in freedom under law and had succeeded in reconciling monarchy with principles of popular sovereignty; all other races, in particular the Celts, required highly centralized or authoritarian institutions in order to prevent violent political and social upheaval. It is important to note that if Victorian Anglo-Saxonists had relatively little occasion to defend their ancient liberties against the absolutist tendencies of their monarch, they did have to contend with what they considered to be a much greater danger to those liberties. This new or assumed threat came from below, not above, that is from the radical and democratic leaders of the increasingly politicized masses. Fear of the levelling and destructive instincts of the working classes, as embodied in Chartist, socialist, and trade unionist organizations, sustained much of the political and social thought of men like Kingsley, Froude, Salisbury, Lecky, and other Victorian opponents of democracy. For these men England's ancient institutions were menaced by Jacobinical survivors of the French revolution, by Luddites and professional agitators who followed the call of Captain Swing or Rebecca in the 1830's and early 1840's or who swallowed the dangerous dogma of Joseph Arch and Joseph Chamberlain in the 1870's and early 1880's.

These dedicated enemies of the free and enlightened institutions which the Saxons or Germans had planted on English shores also had their allies and sympathizers in Ireland where, in the years after 1866 first Fenians and then the followers of Captain Moonlight seemed bent on destroying lives and property as well as the Act of Union by physical force and dynamite. By the early 1880's both Liberal and Conservative leaders were apprehensive lest Parnell's Home Rule movement disrupt the whole parliamentary process at Westminster through systematic obstruction of debate. And the information they received from Ireland contained gruesome accounts of the land war which was forcing landowners and their agents to carry weapons at all times. Well might Anglo-Saxonists in the 1880's denigrate Irish Celtic character in the light of what they read and heard about the criminal brutality of Land League agitators in Ireland. For these reasons it seemed to many educated Englishmen that the Irish Question in its Parnellite phase threatened to undermine such venerable Anglo-Saxon institutions as Parliament and English land law in Ireland. The activities of Parnellites in the House of Commons and their fiery speeches at 'proclaimed' meetings in Ireland, in addition to the crimes committed in the name of the Irish Republican Brotherhood and the Land League, gave Anglo-Saxonists all the excuse they needed to condemn Irishmen as Celts who were incapable of exercising self-control and who were therefore wholly unsuited for self-government by English standards — which were the only ones that counted.

The cult of Anglo-Saxon virtues and the explicit or implied condemnation of Celtic vices constitutes one of the more persistent themes in Victorian novels, poems, and plays, autobiographies, periodicals, and cartoons. One of the best examples of this ethnocentric genre was the periodical called *The Anglo-Saxon* which enjoyed a brief but glorious run in 1849. By way of commemorating the thousandth anniversary of the birth of King Alfred, the editors of this review lavished gushing praise on every form of Anglo-Saxon activity and thought.[25] If *The Anglo-Saxon* lasted no more than a year, the ethnocentric attitudes contained therein lived long after its demise.[26]

In the second half of the nineteenth century many Anglo-Saxonists tried to measure the racial and cultural achievements of the English people in terms of the failure of other races and other cultures to approximate their own standards of success. For this purpose the Celtic race made an excellent yardstick because of its physical and geographical proximity as well as historical connections with the Anglo-Saxons or Teutons, and also because there was no uniform color barrier between the two races that might have complicated the comparison. Wherever one turns in the vast amphitheater of Victorian culture one can find traces of this unequal contest between noble Anglo-Saxons and ignoble Celts. The degree of distortion involved in English attitudes about the Irish Celts varied in direct proportion to the extent of their delusions about both the superiority of English political, legal, social, and religious institutions and the causes of that superiority. This process of distortion resembled in some respects the ways in which Englishmen formed their 'image of Africa' before 1850.[27] In both cases they mixed small fragments of reality with large amounts of what they wanted to believe about the indigenous peoples in order to arrive at a foregone conclusion based on their particular needs at the time.

Most educated Victorians derived their image of Ireland and the Irish either from limited contact with the Irish in Britain or from fiction, memoirs, history books, government reports, 'expert' accounts written by political economists and social reformers, and pure hearsay. In a relatively small number of cases Englishmen could lay claim to firsthand experience, however brief, of the country and its inhabitants. Englishmen who traveled to or through Ireland as tourists, and those who lived there as landlords, administrators, army officers, or businessmen, did not, of course, always agree on what they saw and heard. But they did share in common a tendency to see all things Irish through coated Anglo-Saxon lenses, and their assessments of Irish character usually had a monotonous ring, as though they had made up their minds on the subject even before landing in Ireland. Rare indeed was the English tourist who stepped outside the elegant and well-ordered pale of Anglo-Irish culture to discover 'hidden' or Gaelic Ireland and to savor at close quarters the life and habits of the Irish working classes.[28] By examining the cultural context in which some prominent Englishmen discussed Irish affairs and Irish character, we may be able to judge more accurately the role played by ethnocentric prejudices in shaping the relations of England and Ireland. It is time now to consider some of the distinctions based on racial theories about human behavior which served to divide Anglo-Saxons from Celts in the reign of Queen Victoria.

CHAPTER III

A Tale of Two Races

The gist of many observations made about the Irish people by Victorian Englishmen was that the fundamental differences between English and Irish character were largely, if not exclusively, based on the racial factor. In the conventional language of the day the Celtic blood of the Irish and the Saxon blood of the English determined their contrasting patterns of behavior, and any mixture of the two peoples invariably resulted in the corruption or adulteration of the better (Anglo-Saxon) blood by the baser (Celtic) blood. By the 1850's and 1860's the idea of a sharp dichotomy between the Celts and their derivative tribes on the one hand and the Saxons and their Teutonic or German subdivisions on the other had gained many adherents among European as well as English students of history and scientists of society. Almost all these 'experts' assumed that the Irish were as Celtic a people as one could hope to find in Europe and that the bulk of the modern English were essentially Saxon in their racial makeup.[1] This belief in the contrast between Celts and Anglo-Saxons was held most firmly by those in England and France who were familiar with the racial and ethnological theories of men like the brothers Thierry, William Edwards, Ernest Renan, Count Arthur de Gobineau, and the historian Jules Michelet, whose concern with the rise and fall of races and nations belonged to an intellectual — not to say emotional — tradition that stretched back at least as far as the sixteenth century, when the fascination of English scholars and adventurers with primitive societies and savage men led to the publication of numerous discourses and treatises ranging from pure fantasy to conscientious attempts to understand alien cultures and people.[2]

In the nineteenth century educated Englishmen had access to the latest theories about race and national character which emanated from the Continent not only through the books in which they were contained but also through the media of the established periodicals wherein the works or ideas of prominent French, German, and other foreign writers were often discussed. It was in the pages of the *Quarterly Review,* for example, that some Englishmen were first introduced to the notions of Jules Michelet about the importance of race and national character. In his *History of France* Michelet asserted that the French and the Irish had similar temperaments because they shared in common a large amount of 'Gaelic blood.' The modern descendants of the Gaels, he wrote, not only required "severe preceptors" but also needed to temper their instincts with reason and to act more often on the basis of reflection than impulse. Being something of an ethnocentrist himself, Michelet could not resist the temptation of asserting that "the genius of the free personality" was far more a Celtic than a German characteristic.[3]

The doctrine of conflict and antithesis between the races of mankind loomed much larger in the writings of Count Arthur de Gobineau, whose *Essay on the Inequality of the Human Races,* first published in 1853, became one of the most influential books ever written on the subject of race.[4] Gobineau began his famous inquiry with the conviction that "the race question dominates all the other problems of history, that it holds the key to them, and that the inequality of races from whose fusion a people is formed is enough to explain the whole course of its destiny." One of the most pessimistic of all nineteenth-century conservatives, Gobineau was obsessed with the decline of those once noble races, among others the Frankish nobility in France, who had been the real architects of Western European civilization. An insecure aristocrat embittered by his own social irrelevance in an increasingly egalitarian world, he insisted that the inequality of races as well as classes sufficed to explain the rise and fall of civilizations. From his study of elite races in the past he arrived at the conclusion that it was neither fanaticism, luxury, corruption, irreligion, nor the absence of great men that had caused their decay or collapse, but rather the conflict of races and classes and the concomitant "adulteration" of the blood which flowed through the veins of those concerned. Starting with the hypothesis that there were "serious and ultimate differences of value" between and among human races, he ended by arguing that the mixing of races was both unnatural and yet inevitable. Although history had proven that an "irreconcilable antagonism" prevailed between the races of man, there were nevertheless certain elements of attraction between and among them. For Gobineau the "innate repulsion" of the races served as both cause and effect of racial inequality. He perceived or constructed a world of separate yet interacting because competing, racial units, a world in which war, invasion, and colonization acted as the most forceful agents of miscegenation. Mankind was one vast hierarchy in which there were always some forces at work tending for better or worse to mix those races nearest one another.[5]

Gobineau's triadic division of mankind into the White, Yellow, and Black races, each with its own set of traits and values, reflected the association which Europeans had made for centuries between skin color or pigmentation and behavioral traits. The White races were, needless to say, far superior to the others, especially in intelligence and the instinct for order.[6] The Yellow races were deficient in ambition, imagination, and physical strength, but in all important respects they surpassed the Black or negroid races, which were notable for their animal sensuality and emotional instability. Gobineau was, of course, too French and too cosmopolitan to subscribe to Anglo-Saxonist mythology, so he placed the Celtic peoples on a par with the Slavonic, Germanic, Hellenic and other peoples in his White category. At the same time he did insist that the large scale migrations and emigrations of the working classes from all over Europe, including Ireland, posed a serious threat to the purity, and therefore to the ascendancy, of the Anglo-Saxon race. The ambivalence of Gobineau's theories about the constant interaction of races emerges clearly from his argument that some mixture of blood not only does take place, especially at the margins or boundaries where races overlap, but that this process of hybridization had determined the rise and decline of every important civilization in the past. More aware of the paradoxical play of attraction and repulsion in the relations of the races than some of his critics allowed, Gobineau indulged his fantasies in trying to build a pattern of rising and falling civilizations, the cycles of each being determined by the degree of hybridization at work.

Gobineau, the racial determinist and Aryan apologist, was also an elitist who declared that the civilization of a composite people like the French did not permeate or characterize all the classes therein. In the case of France there were quite distinct racial and cultural influences at work in the various social strata, and he contended that the "directing forces of the national culture" had not percolated down to the working classes in the country. Gobineau ended his treatise with an admonition to his readers that every possible precaution ought to be taken to ensure the preservation of the noble and civilized Aryan races. Although he was too pessimistic to believe that his warning would be taken seriously by many of his contemporaries, he lived long enough to see his ideas quoted by ethnologists and publicists of race thinking in England and on the Continent. The *Essay on Inequality* achieved notoriety largely because the racial determinists of subsequent generations, especially in Germany, chose to direct his racist and elitist theories against a specific target, primarily, but not exclusively, against the Jews. To this extent Gobineau's views were distorted and abused in somewhat the same way that social Darwinists perverted the *Origin of Species* in order to suit their own needs and ends. Gobineau's ideas fed on the fears and frustrations of many Europeans who were caught up in the personal and collective trials of rapid industrialization and urbanization, with their concomitants of increasing class consciousness, social tensions, and conspicuous social mobility. The idea of racial determinism, with its elitist or caste component as supplied by Gobineau, seemed to provide a scientific basis for the resentment felt by many educated persons against those classes, out-groups, or races which were, in their subjective opinion, eroding or challenging the old, traditional society epitomized by their own in-group.

In the mid-nineteenth century there was another Frenchman whose ethnological views reached the English educated classes through periodicals and books, even if those views did not have the same impact on Englishmen, Matthew Arnold excepted, as did Gobineau's essay. Apart from his commitment to the idea of race as shaping human behavior, Ernest Renan had little in common with Gobineau. Renan was both more optimistic and less apocalyptic than his elitist contemporary about the destiny of the races of man. Just as Gobineau believed that he had a mission to save what was left of the ascendancy of the white, Aryan races, so Renan saw as his task the redemption or rehabilitation of the Celtic people. In 1854 he published his revealing treatise, *La Poèsie des Races Celtiques,* which stands as something of a landmark in the development of a Celticist self-image resilient enough to ward off the blows of Anglo-Saxonists in England and Teutonists in Germany.[7]

Far from being a closely reasoned study of Welsh, Irish, Cornish, or Breton poetry, this essay was merely a vehicle for Renan's conviction that the two races represented by the Celts and the Teutons were utterly at odds in terms of blood and character. Not only was there a wide gap between them, but the Celts possessed a purity of blood and an integrity of character that could not be matched by any other race in the world. Renan's image of the Celts, however, did not lack a critical element. He did not deny the presence of some faults in this gifted people who were unique in their isolation from the other races of Europe. Indeed, the Celts' "powerful personality" was responsible for their hatred of all foreigners and for their refusal to accept modern civilization. Unfortunately, too, the Celt lacked a sense of reality and had no desire to expand his racial and cultural boundaries, aggression and conquest being entirely foreign to his nature. The trouble with the modern Celt, according to Renan, was that he had allowed civilization to pass him by because he preferred to maintain close family ties rather than to construct abstract theories of sovereignty. The Celtic race had no real aptitude for politics largely because the overpowering spirit of the family had stifled all attempts to attain more complex social and political organization.

Renan lamented the passing of the glorious achievements of the Celtic people who were now incapable of progressing by their own unaided efforts. They were a shy and retiring, a sad and timid race. Most of them were also sober, but that sobriety did not extend to the Breton and Irish Celts, for whom drunkenness served as the only means of experiencing both vividly and frequently the inner world of dreams, illusions, and fantasies which was so important to them. Renan went on to describe the Celts as essentially feminine. No race had ever invested love with so much mystery, had ever conceived the ideal of woman with greater delicacy, or had ever been more completely dominated by that ideal. The Celt's worship of woman was a sort of "intoxication, a madness, a vertigo."[8] The Celts were, in sum, a retiring, proud, delicate, sentimental, imaginative race — a people "neither sad nor gay, ever in suspense between a smile and a tear."[9] What made them such a noble race was not just their sensitivity but their commitment to justice, loyalty, and sympathy which Renan found mirrored in all their early heroic poems.

Such lyrical, indeed ecstatic, views about the Celts were heard more often in the British Isles after the founding of the Gaelic League and various Irish literary societies in the early 1890's, but in mid-Victorian England they were shared by very few persons, not forgetting the notable Lady Charlotte Schreiber (Guest) who had edited the great Welsh epic, *The Mabinogion,* between 1838 and 1849. English friends of the Celts and Celtic culture were few and far between, and they lacked a spokesman of Renan's stature and gift for eulogy until the mid-1860's. By all counts the most articulate and forceful statement by any Victorian about the aesthetic and emotional disparities of Celt and Saxon came from Matthew Arnold, who gave four lectures at Oxford in 1865-66. First published in the *Cornhill* in 1866 and then in book form under the title *On the Study of Celtic Literature,* these famous lectures amounted to much more than a plea for the creation of a chair of Celtic studies at Oxford in order to end the ignorance of centuries in English universities about Celtic literature and culture.[10] Arnold had been impressed by the work of German scholars like J. K. Zeuss, author of *Grammatica Celtica* (1851), and Francis Bopp, who had applied scientific methods to the study of Celtic philology, literature, and artifacts, and he wanted to see English scholars of the same caliber working to remove the prejudices and legends which surrounded this body of literature. If Arnold's ostensible purpose in these lectures was to promote disinterested research into Celtic culture, his underlying object was to differentiate between and among the various racial elements which went to make up what he considered to be English literature as well as English character.

When viewed against a background of chronic unrest in Ireland as well as against a foreground of massive indifference in some cases, and actual hostility in others, to all things Celtic, Arnold's lectures look much more like a study of national or racial character in the British Isles than an analysis of a body of literature, most of which he had never read in the original languages. Arnold could rightly claim that he knew more about the subject than any of his English contemporaries, but that 'more' was not as much as he wished his audience to believe. When one considers the mixture of literary speculation, ethnological myth, and sporadic insight in this essay, it is all the more curious that no Irish or English critic managed to demolish his interpretation either in his own lifetime or for years thereafter. And it is also remarkable that Arnold's notions about the ingredients of Celtic genius, which were derived in large part from Renan, should have had such a strong appeal to many of the leading figures in the Irish literary revival.[11]

In the course of his introductory remarks Arnold told his audience that when he surveyed the England of his day, he found among the many discontents and injustices, which he liked to blame on the Philistinism of the middle classes, a deep-seated antipathy toward the Celtic peoples of Wales, Scotland, and Ireland. Deploring this animosity and suspicion, he entered a plea for mutual understanding and acceptance between Saxons and Celts in the British Isles, and he went out of his way to insist that such understanding ought to be specially directed toward the Irish in view of the poverty and unrest in Ireland. Turning from the theme of conciliation for Ireland to his main topic, namely the ethnic and emotional makeup of the modern English people, he explained the need for the creation of a new unity out of the mixed or hybrid heritage of the British people. With "scientific" objectivity he then proceeded to separate and identify the specifically Celtic, German, and Norman ingredients in English character as well as literature. This attempt to isolate the racial elements in English blood and artistic achievement did not seem at all ludicrous to his audience, most of whom were evidently convinced that race had a vital role to play in shaping the literature as well as temperament of any people. Arnold insisted that the diverse traits of these three racial groups had been blended over the centuries in the person of the Englishman — a generic term for what he held to be a hybrid stock.

Some of Arnold's ethnic attitudes may be explained by his father's firm conviction that there was an "impassable gulf" between Saxon and Celt. Dr. Arnold was the kind of Anglo-Saxonist who not only felt contempt for Celts, but taught his children to believe that the differences between Saxon and Celt were far greater than those between the Saxons and any other race in the world. And he did not mince his words on the subject: the Celts, he declared, were notorious for their idleness, dishonesty, savagery, and brutality.[12] When Matthew Arnold reached manhood, he began to chafe against his father's strictures about the Celts, but his filial rebellion was never complete, and as a result his interpretation of Celtic and Saxon character remained ambiguous and even inconsistent.[13] Because Arnold was not an Anglo-Saxonist like his father, he contended that the past difference between the two races should not be allowed to obscure either their shared Indo-European features or the degree to which their spirits had become fused in the person of the archetypal Englishman. By incorporating into his study some of the latest findings of philologists and ethnologists about the links connecting the various Indo-European races, Arnold was able to discern a greater unity between Celt and Saxon than the disparities of their two 'geniuses' would suggest. Besides his indebtedness to Zeuss and Bopp and to the distinguished Irish scholar, Eugene O'Curry, Arnold owed a great deal of his inspiration to Renan's essay on Celtic poetry, even though he believed that Renan had carried the glorification of the Celt too far. Renan's failure to appreciate either Irish literature or Irish character had, in fact, spurred Arnold to search for a more universal formula to explain Celtic 'genius.'

Arnold began his analysis of English 'genius' by describing it as "energy with honesty"; and this was closely related to German genius, which was "steadiness with honesty." But there was too much of the "humdrum, the plain and ugly, the ignoble" about German genius. The Saxon was neither agreeable nor dynamic. He quoted from an old Irish poem the well-known lines:

> For dulness, the creeping Saxons;
> For beauty and amorousness, the Gaedhils.[14]

And with this ancient text in mind he embarked on a revealing description of Celtic genius, the chief feature of which was sentiment. His own words on the subject of Celtic character are worth quoting:

> An organisation quick to feel impressions, and feeling them very strongly; a lively personality therefore, keenly sensitive to

joy and to sorrow; this is the main point. If the downs of life too much outnumber the ups, this temperament, just because it is so quickly and nearly conscious of all impressions, may no doubt be seen shy and wounded; it may be seen in wistful regret, it may be seen in passionate, penetrating melancholy; but its essence is to aspire ardently after life, light, and emotion, to be expansive, adventurous, and gay. . . . The Celt is often called sensual; but it is not so much the vulgar satisfactions of sense that attract him as emotion and excitement; he is truly . . . sentimental.[15]

Arnold found the key to Celtic character in the readiness to react or revolt against "the despotism of fact" — an idea he had borrowed from the French historian, Henri Martin. It was this reaction that accounted for the Celt's "habitual want of success." The Celt had always lacked "balance, measure, and patience." Despite his gifts of "quick perception" and "warm emotion," he had never achieved perfection in art because he had none of the German's steadiness and sanity. The Celt was a prisoner of his own emotions. Impatience and instability prevented him from accomplishing anything in the way of great works of art and literature. For Arnold the Celt's "infinite sentiment" robbed him of both spiritual and material achievement; and his aversion to the despotism of fact "lamed him in the world of business and politics."[16]

If Arnold perceived a number of Celtic faults, the full length portrait was not unflattering because he was convinced that the Celt possessed many of the components of the ideal genius. The gifts of the Celt complemented those of the German and the Latinized Norman. The Celts supplied the spark, the dynamic quality, and the sensibility, all of which blended with German steadiness and Norman respect for fact and political talents to make the English character. Within the Englishman and his literature there was a rough equilibrium between the spiritual qualities of the Celts with their sensitivity to "natural magic" and the more practical, rational gifts of the German and Norman. Arnold thus tried to reconcile the disparate features of Celt, German, and Norman in his concept of the English genius. The Englishman, he argued, could not do without any of these ingredients, least of all those that were Celtic. He drew his lectures to a close with a statesmanlike appeal, worthy of Mill or Gladstone, to every Englishman to send "through the gentle ministration of science, a message of peace to Ireland."[17]

Oxford established a chair of Celtic studies in 1877, but the mutual understanding between England and Ireland for which Arnold pleaded did not come about in his lifetime. Arnold himself had no trouble in deciding to oppose Home Rule in 1886. Not only did he question the political capacity of Irishmen in his later writings but he argued that the Irish were insubordinate, idle, and improvident. Admittedly he held England responsible for much of Ireland's misery, but his plea for judging the Celt without prejudice went further in word than in deed. In Arnold's view it was one thing to appreciate Celtic genius, and quite another matter to surrender the Act of Union to the demands of a ravenous Irish party led by Parnell in the House of Commons.[18]

Arnold's attempt to treat Celtic character sympathetically provoked some acid comments in the *Times* about the folly of Eisteddfods and the futility of the Welsh language revival: a few experts questioned his views about Celtic literature in general and Macpherson's *Ossian* in particular; and the inauspicious timing of the lectures' publication, coinciding as it did with Fenian outbreaks of violence in Ireland and England, moved some Englishmen to wonder whether sensibility or dynamite was the more accurate expression of Irish Celtic character. Arnold's sentimental ethnology converted only those who wished to be converted, and the bulk of the Victorian intelligentsia paid more attention to *Culture and Anarchy* than to the *Study of Celtic Literature*.

For the Anglo-Saxonists of this period a far more important work than Arnold's essay on national or racial character was Charles Dilke's *Greater Britain*, published in 1868.[19] Here the idea of racial antithesis and conflict loomed large, and there was evidence to spare for the believer in a fundamental struggle between Saxons and Irish Celts. This book was the more remarkable because it had been written by a mere youth, the son of one of the promoters of the Great Exhibition, who had decided to spend the year following his graduation from Cambridge travelling around the world. The young Dilke was fascinated by the extraordinary achievements of the Anglo-Saxon people, and he chose to search for the causes of their success in every important part of that far-flung community which he called "Greater

Britain" or "Saxondom." Dilke's mind was saturated with notions about racial distinctions and antipathies. "Love of race among the English," he wrote, "rests upon a firmer base than either love of mankind or love of Britain, for it reposes upon a subsoil of things known: the ascertained virtues and powers of the English people."[20] Memories of Charles Kingsley's stirring lectures on the exploits of Saxon or English heroes in medieval England still lingered in his mind. What inspired Dilke through all his travels was a vision of "the grandeur of our race" — a race destined to rule and to spread itself over all the earth. Blood was stronger than political ties, national boundaries, or trade agreements. British power and influence did not stop at the edges of the formal empire but spilled over into every region of the world where Anglo-Saxons had settled.

Dilke was a racial imperialist who revered the blood and institutions that bound together Anglo-Saxons throughout the world; the informal empire he recognized was based on blood not trade. His description of America is significant for what it says about the mixture and collision of races there: America was a vast battleground on which the "dearer" and the "cheaper" races were waging an all-out war for supremacy. By the "dearer" races he meant in the first instance the Anglo-Saxons and also the Scandinavian and German peoples. The "cheaper" races were the Irish and the Chinese — both prolific breeders, hard workers, and inveterate migrants. Dilke even described the Chinese as the Irish of the Orient. What was at stake in this struggle between the principal races of the world was not just the material wealth of America but the survival of Anglo-Saxon civilization. The Irish in America were like the swelling waters of a flood threatening to blot out the Anglo-Saxon landscape. They were gradually taking over New York City and parts of Boston and Philadelphia. In the near future all the great American cities would be Irish while the countryside would remain English.[21] It was the fate of Anglo-Saxons and their culture that troubled him; he could face the prospect of the vanishing tribes of American Indians with equanimity. "The gradual extinction of the inferior races," he declared, "is not only a law of nature, but a blessing to mankind."[22]

Fascinated by the racial antagonism he encountered in America between whites and Negroes in the south, Irish and English in the north and east, and between Chinese and whites in the far west,

Dilke wondered at times where this incessant collision would end. He did not lose heart because of his unshakable faith in the superior qualities of the Anglo-Saxon race. Nature, he observed, had intended the English to be a race of officers whose task was "to direct and guide the cheap labor of the Eastern peoples."[23] There seemed to be no limits to the future of the Anglo-Saxon race which was marching westward through America and across the Pacific on the way to "universal rule". The Anglo-Saxons were, after all, the only extirpating race on earth. They had decimated the Indians of North America, the Maoris of New Zealand, and the aborigines of Australia. If Dilke was not wholly consistent on the subject of racial mixture, if he hedged on the question of miscegenation between conquerors and conquered, he remained convinced that the virile Anglo-Saxons would eventually "rise triumphant from the doubtful struggle" against the "cheaper" races.[24] Pride in race and belief in the genius of the English as supreme colonizers and rulers, warriors, and traders animated Dilke's book, and a talent for description of both the people and natural beauty he encountered made it immensely readable. What appealed most to his English readers was his optimism about the ultimate victory of the Anglo-Saxon race over the "cheaper" races of the world. America, Dilke wrote, offered the English race "the moral directorship of the globe, by ruling mankind through Saxon institutions and the English tongue. Through America, England is speaking to the world."[25] And through his book Dilke was exhorting the Anglo-Saxon people to be on their guard against the encroachment of "inferior" or "cheaper" races like the Irish and to recognize their mission to spread Anglo-Saxon civilization around the world.

The idea of a dichotomy between Celt and Saxon was used by many other Victorians besides Dilke to convey a sense of racial conflict between the two that was never intended by Arnold. In the periodical literature there are many examples of that "impassable gulf" between these two races. The *Edinburgh Review*, which was generally less susceptible to racial doctrines than most other periodicals, described Ireland and Great Britain in 1846 as "among the most dissimilar nations in Europe. They differ in race, in religion, in civilisation, and in wealth."[26] The reviewer of W. S. Trench's book, *Realities of Irish Life* (1868) in the *Quarterly Review* pointed out that it was foolish for the political economists to prescribe remedies

for the Irish question until the character of the Irish people had completely changed. J. S. Mill's mistake, he maintained, was to treat Irish
cottiers as though they were Englishmen. It was time Mill learned
that the Irishman was "not an average human being — an idiomatic
and idiosyncratic, not an abstract, man."[27] Phrases like the "permanent conditions of human nature" and "historic antipathies of race"
occurred frequently in articles on Irish subjects appearing in the
Quarterly, and most of its reviewers stressed the importance of national or racial character in promoting agitation and disorder in Ireland.[28]

Such were a few of the theories and beliefs available to those
Englishmen who had to pass judgment on Irish questions in the last
quarter of the century. There are many other examples of those
theories about the antithesis of Saxon and Celt, some of which appear below. But what they had in common was the assumption that
racial differences and the inequalities stemming from them were
facts of life and that the character of a people was more or less biologically determined and could not be changed without prolonged
crossbreeding or miscegenation. However much disagreement and
inconsistency there was among Englishmen about the effects of mixing Celtic and Saxon blood, almost all Anglo-Saxonists agreed that
the Irish Celt occupied a rung considerably below themselves on the
ladder of human races.

CHAPTER IV

The Importance of Being Paddy

Like all images of other people, nations, and cultures the English image of Ireland and the Irish in the middle and later decades of the nineteenth century was a composite or mosaic made up of many different impressions and degrees of familiarity with the country and its inhabitants. But the diversity of sources from which Anglo-Saxonists drew their 'facts' did not prevent their image of the Irish from hardening into a more or less rigid category to which there were no exceptions that mattered. Out of the wealth or welter of observations about Ireland and its people which the Victorians have left behind it is possible to detect certain patterns of thinking among the adjectives and descriptive phrases which were repeated over and over again. These adjectives served as the bricks with which the English house of anti-Irish prejudice was built. The composition and quality of these bricks as well as the type of mortar used to hold them together must now be examined in order to arrive at some understanding of why there was such fierce opposition to Irish Home Rule in England. The significance of the English stereotype of Irish character — better known as 'Paddy' — has been ignored by most modern historians of Anglo-Irish relations, and this neglect may account for the obscurity which surrounds the reasons for the failure of English policy in Ireland.

One of the first things to be noted about English images of Ireland is the rapidity and ease with which they were formed. No one familiar with the dynamics of prejudice will be surprised to learn that images of the Irish were often constructed out of the flimsiest of materials. When John Ruskin paid his first visit to Ireland in August, 1861, he wrote that Dublin was "far the melancholiest place" he had ever seen, and then added:

> What I have seen of the Irish themselves in just the two hours after landing, like one's first impression of Calais — will, I suppose, remain as the permanent impression. I had no conception the stories of Ireland were so true. I had fancied all were violent exaggeration. But it is impossible to exaggerate.[1]

Ruskin did in fact discover some agreeable traits in Irishmen, but many of his English contemporaries decided on equally scanty evidence that the Irish had few if any redeeming features. In Victorian England prejudice against Irish Celts could be found in forms both subtle and blatant. Sir William Hart Dyke had been Irish Chief Secretary for only a few months in 1885, when he came to realize the degree of hostility towards Ireland and the Irish among the politicians he encountered at Westminster. He wrote to Lord Carnarvon, the Irish Viceroy, that he had found in the Conservative Party "the same hopeless indifference and ignorance in every quarter, plus an amount of prejudice, which would drive John Bright wild with envy."[2] Another Tory Chief Secretary, Walter Long, who prided himself on his knowledge of Ireland, tried to warn the government about the extent of disloyalty in Ireland after the outbreak of war in 1914. In a letter to the Permanent Under Secretary at Dublin Castle, Sir Matthew Nathan, written in 1915, he argued that anti-Irish prejudices could not be lightly dismissed: "I confess I don't see any chance myself of an early decease of these old, but well-founded, prejudices. The great thing to remember is that their foundation is *fact* and not imagination and therefore they will be very difficult to remove."[3]

Many of the most striking examples of prejudice against the Irish in nineteenth-century England may be found among the members of the English governing classes and in the papers they read like the *Times* and the *Morning Post*. A good illustration of this point is the letter Disraeli wrote to the *Times* in April, 1836 denouncing the Lichfield House compact in bitter terms. The Irish, he wrote:

> hate our free and fertile isle. They hate our order, our civilisation, our enterprising industry, our sustained courage, our deco-

rous liberty, our pure religion. This wild, reckless, indolent, uncertain and superstitious race have no sympathy with the English character. Their fair ideal of human felicity is an alternation of clannish broils and coarse idolatry. Their history describes an unbroken circle of bigotry and blood.[4]

Of the many pejorative adjectives applied by educated Englishmen to the Irish perhaps the most damaging, certainly the most persistent, were those which had to do with their alleged unreliability, emotional instability, mental disequilibrium, or dualistic temperament. The stereotypical Irishman was a kind of Celtic Jekyll and Hyde; he oscillated between two extremes of behavior and mood; he was liable to rush from mirth to despair, tenderness to violence, and loyalty to treachery. The Irish were therefore often treated as an untrustworthy and dishonest people. When Edward Hamilton announced to his family his intention of going to Ireland in 1873, his uncle wrote at once advising him not to bring back an Irish wife: "The whole nation lies and that is not a good quality in a wife."[5] Several years later Hamilton received another lecture from his uncle about Ireland:

> I have never been in Ireland & I dislike the Irish so much that I have never made an effort to extend my sphere of knowledge in that direction. But one ought to see & learn — & it is only by personal observation that one can form sound conclusions about the many questions which are perpetually worrying Parliament in reference to that ill-fated country.[6]

It was this distrust and suspicion of the Irish that continued to warp Anglo-Irish relations well into the twentieth century. Sir Garnet Wolseley, another case in point, thought he knew just how to deal with 'Paddy.' Despite his Anglo-Irish ancestry Wolseley considered himself a Saxon and as such far superior to the Irish Celt. He contended that Irishmen behaved only when they had been made to recognize the superior power and intelligence of the Saxon. The Irishman, Wolseley wrote, "soon takes his hat off when he finds a master who is not afraid of him and who is always ready to tackle him." He found the bulk of the Irish people physically repellant, describing them as men "with noses so cut away that you can see the place where their brains should be. . . . They are a strange, illogical, inaccurate race, with the most amiable qualities, garnished with the dirt and squalor which they seem to love as dearly as their religion."[7] Caricatures of this kind were quite common among the dominant military caste in Irish society, most of whose members were more than conscious of the 'Irish blood' in their veins.

Throughout the nineteenth century the prevalent English stereotype of the Irish Celt underwent only slight changes in detail, while the overall profile changed only in the sense that it became sharper in focus. The epitome of that stereotype was 'Paddy,' who was really an invention of the early Victorian imagination, although the word itself goes back in English literature at least to Arthur Young's *Tour in Ireland,* published in 1780.[8] 'Paddy' was at first primarily a figure of fun and even affection for some Englishmen. He was usually a feckless, devil-may-care, rollicking, hard-drinking, and hard-fighting peasant who posed a more serious threat to himself and those with whom he lived than to Irish landlords and English officials. Paddy was, however, something more than a derivative of the stage Irishman who had cavorted in English plays for at least two centuries.[9] The name connoted other things to Victorians besides an ignorant laborer full of blarney and drink, laughter and tears. Paddy also meant a temper tantrum and was occasionally used to describe "the choleric reputation of the Irish." The word 'Irish' itself had a number of derogatory meanings: to "weep Irish" meant to feign sorrow (crocodile tears); to "go to an Irish wedding" was also an expression for emptying a cesspool; to "get up one's Irish" meant, of course, to display one's anger or *ire*.[10] As the Irish people became more politically aware and organized in the course of the nineteenth century, Paddy began to lose some of his humorous and innocuous qualities and gradually acquired instead those attributes which well educated and respectable Englishmen were taught never to display in public. Taken in conjunction with the spread of racial explanations of human behavior, the stereotype of Paddy grew steadily in social and political significance because it embodied not only a collection of highly undesirable traits but a permanent condition or state of mind and body according to the laws of racial inheritance. The presence of these reprehensible features in Paddy made him all the less eligible in

English eyes for the concessions which his leaders in Parliament were demanding from the British government.

What then were the main ingredients of the ever hardening stereotpye of Irish character in the Victorian period? Reduced to its barest and most often heard essentials, Paddy was made up of the following adjectives: childish, emotionally unstable, ignorant, indolent, superstitious, primitive or semi-civilized, dirty, vengeful, and violent. That Paddy could also be amusing, likeable — at a distance — and loyal to the Crown did not, of course, invalidate the stereotype and did not make him any more fit for self-government in English eyes.[11] Those Englishmen who accepted the existence of Paddy as a collective entity tended to believe that the Anglo-Saxons possessed traits exactly opposite to those that made the Irish Celt so unfit for the management of his own affairs. Where the Celt was child-like, the Anglo-Saxon was mature; instead of emotional instability, he could boast of self-control; he was energetic not lazy, rational not superstitious, civilized not primitive, clean not dirty, ready to forgive not vengeful, and prepared to live under the rule of law. This temperamental antithesis was all-embracing: it left no loophole for the Irish to share much in common with their English rulers.

One of the favorite ascriptions of Englishmen and women about the Irish concerned their childlike qualities. Summing up her impressions of a week's tour in the west of Ireland, Edith Balfour, who married Alfred Lyttelton, observed:

> They are like children still listening to old fairy stories while their bread has to be earned; they are like children who are afraid to walk alone, who play with fire, who are helpless; like children who will not grow up.
>
> But, like children too, they have a strange ancient wisdom and an innate purity, and they appeal to the love and the pity of all who come in contact with them.
>
> What would I not give . . . to help them? But the task is very difficult, and if you give children complete freedom they will certainly stray.[12]

Walter Long supplied another example of this attitude when he wrote to Sir Matthew Nathan in December, 1914, urging him to take a tough line against the publication of seditious literature in Ireland. All past experience of the Irish, he argued, went to prove that the only thing they really understood was "a strong, unflinching" government. Once they saw that disloyalty went unpunished they naturally misbehaved. "It is not because they really want to do mischief," Long declared, "so much as like naughty children, they think it is amusing to give way to their inclinations."[13] The Countess of Leitrim took the same view during the great war when recruiting drives in the west of Ireland were producing meager rseults. The Irish, she argued, needed compulsory recruitment because, "In so many ways they are like children & they don't understand an invitation where they would quietly obey an *order*."[14] Irishmen thus shared with virtually all the nonwhite peoples of the empire the label of childish, and the remedy for unruly children in most Victorian households was a proper 'licking.'[15]

The charge of instability or emotional incontinence played such an important role in the English image of the Irish Celt that it deserves a closer look. By instability English observers meant that the Irish not only lived by and off their irrational impulses but experienced rapid alternation of moods or emotions. Here again the self-image of the Anglo-Saxon came into play, for emotional restraint or continence was that quality most highly prized for economic as well as moral reasons among the respectable members of the middle and upper classes. And those Englishmen who were trying to become respectable had Samuel Smiles to remind them that self-control and disciplined character were the chief attributes of England's greatest heroes.[16] Of all the Irishman's traits his reputation for emotionalism was perhaps the most damning so far as estimates of his political capacities were concerned. This idea was expressed in many different ways by the Victorians and their successors. Tennyson's stanza in *In Memoriam,* "the blind hysterics of the Celt" comes first to mind. The *Edinburgh Review* in 1834 drew attention to the striking contrasts in Irish character as seen in the "strongest sympathy for distress" on the one hand, and a "desperate recklessness of the consequences of actions" and "a spirit of revenge, not to be satiated except by blood" on the other.[17] The same periodical remarked in 1852 on "that strange mixture of strong passion and playfulness, of the solemn and the ludicrous" which was so prominent a part of

Irish character.[18] In spite of their "high qualities," the Irish were "unhappily distinguished by a capricious instability of national temper, which time has but little modified."[19] Dr. B. W. Richardson told an audience at the Denbigh Eisteddfod in 1882 that the Irish were an intensely emotional people: "They are easily cast down, easily elated . . . hopeful on one side, desponding on the other, and at different times hopeful and desponding on the self-same subject."[20] Mrs. S. C. Hall in her *Tales of Irish Life and Character*, based on extensive tours in Ireland in the 1830's, wrote that "The tear and the smile, as regards Ireland, seem really twin-born: the one invariably accompanies the other. Like its native music, the feeling it excites is of mingled joy and gloom." The Irish, Mrs. Hall continued, were "the children of impulse: a single idea fixes itself upon their imaginations and from that they act."[21] Victorian works of fiction contain many illustrations of this theme of Irish emotional instability. Take for example Kipling's picture of the impulsive and passionate Private Mulvaney in *Plain Tales from the Hills*, George Meredith's volatile Captain Con O'Donnell in *Celt and Saxon*, the pathetic, suicidal Boucher in Mrs. Gaskell's *North and South*, or the split personality of Lord Kilgobbin in Charles Lever's novel of that name.

The political significance of this attribution of polarity and ambivalence in Irish character lay in the view shared by many Englishmen that the Irish really did not know what they wanted in the way of political institutions. Unionists contended that the Irish people had no strong convictions about Home Rule and lacked the staying power to keep such an agitation alive for any length of time. As the *Quarterly Review* solemnly declared in 1893, the agitation for Home Rule would burst like a bubble once Gladstone had been removed from public life.[22] The majority of Irishmen were the dupes of professional agitators, so the argument went, who were promising endless miracles once a national parliament had been set up in Dublin. The view that Irishmen lived in a state of alternating tears and laughter was less innocent than it might at first appear, for the conclusion drawn from this belief was that the pendulum-like nature of Irish emotions disqualified them from having any real voice in their government; and it might even be argued that this image helped to implement as well as justify those alternating currents of English policy in Ireland, coercion and conciliation.

As to Paddy's proverbial ignorance, little need be added on this score because the Irish were supposed to share the educational and intellectual deficiencies of almost all peasants or agricultural laborers in Roman Catholic societies. According to the English stereotype the Irish Celts were dreamers and brooders not seekers after facts; their illiteracy caused them to be kept in ignorance by their priests who wanted to enhance their own influence. Every Irishman, quipped Augustus Hare, had a potato in his head. Even Charles Lever, who was not altogether unsympathetic to the Irish people, described the tenantry in one of his novels as so ignorant that they did not know the meaning of the word evicted.[23] In the 1880's most Tories regarded the Irish as utterly gullible when listening to the preachings of priests and the harangues of Parnellite or republican agitators. Ignorance and its companion, superstition, made them blind to the realities of politics and economics; it also encouraged in them a tendency to deal in outrageous exaggeration or 'blarney.'

Among the champions of Anglo-Saxonism there was virtually unanimous agreement about the indolence of the Irish Celts. The image of the lazy Irishman was an ancient one, dating well before the late sixteenth and early seventeenth centuries when Fynes Moryson, Lithgow, the Scottish pilgrim, and other travelers in Ireland noticed the unusual degree of slothfulness and 'sluggishness' shown by the people.[24] Swift found that in most parts of the country the Irish were from infancy "so given up to idleness and sloth" that they often preferred to beg or steal rather than work for a wage.[25] Arthur Young deplored the idleness he saw on his tour in 1776: the people were lazy when it came to work but keen and agile in playing games.[26] Tourists in Ireland habitually remarked on the indolence of the people who never seemed to exert themselves in agricultural or industrial pursuits. Why else should the method of growing potatoes be known as the "lazy bed" system? The *Quarterly Review* in 1849 quoted the remark that the Irishman's "hereditary indolence" made him readier to take up arms in rebellion than a spade.[27] Arriving in Cork in 1842, Thackeray was amazed by the crowd of rascals, rogues, and beggars that swirled around his coach. "Have they nothing else to do," he asked, " — or is it that they *will* do nothing but starve, swagger and be idle in the streets?" At Skibberreen he noted "the ragged lazy contentment" of the people and especially the children, who seemed to have nothing better to do than wait for the arrival of the next coach.[28] English tourists in Ireland also found that idleness characterized the 'squireens' or petty landowners. This class appeared to regard idleness as a sign of gentility, and Arthur Young condemned their preference for "drinking, wrangling, quarreling, fighting, ravishing, etc." Many Englishmen thought that Ireland's greatest need was industry, not in the sense of industrialization such as had transformed Great Britain, but habits of industriousness. When applied to Ireland, the word industry took on a more moral and less material meaning. It connoted exertion, ambition to improve one's lot, prudence, and frugality. Ireland, it was argued, did not need factories and machines so much as a working class willing to live by the code of Samuel Smiles and ready to break the habit of leaning perpetually on spades or on state assistance. A moral rather than an industrial revolution was in order.[29]

Squalor was another feature of Irish life that had bulked large in the English image of Ireland for centuries. By common English consent the Irish did not know the difference between dirt and cleanliness. There is scarcely a description of Ireland in the Victorian era without its set passage on the dirt, misery, and primitiveness of the Irish cabin or rural dwelling. English tourists rarely failed to notice the pile of dung outside the door, the absence of ventilation and light inside, the dirt floor and shallow trench separating human and animal life, the filthy pile of straw on which the entire family slept, the pot used for cooking and storage of potatoes, the fetid smell of people and pigs living together in cramped quarters, the adults dressed in patched clothing, the children in rags and as likely as not half naked and barefoot.[30] This stock picture of squalor in the Irish countryside must have served to distract attention from the grinding poverty and sordid conditions which prevailed in English cities and towns as well as in many rural communities. Ireland did not need a Chadwick to publicize the extent of dirt and disease in both towns and countryside. But only a Carlyle was capable of painting an unforgettable picture of Irish squalor and degradation, while at the same time angrily denouncing the "Demon of Mechanism" and the new poor law which made such savage animals out of the "finest peasantry in the world."[31]

Irish squalor also encouraged the symbolic representation of the

Irish people by the pig. To Englishmen the ubiquitous pig, allegedly an intimate member of every rural Irish household and vital sector of the family's domestic economy, made a most appropriate symbol. English cartoonists took delight in using pigs to represent Paddy and the Irish parliamentary party. Augustine Birrell was particularly fond of the metaphor and used it on more than one occasion in his correspondence with Nathan to depict the inhabitants of a country which he found both "hateful & fascinating."[32] The porcine symbol was more than a cartoonist's convenience. It was a shorthand method of conveying just those brutish, primitive, and dirty qualities which were associated with the vast majority of Irishmen.

To Englishmen of the middle and upper classes who were increasingly self-conscious about public sanitation and personal hygiene, the squalor of Irish life meant not only that the country was uncivilized but that the people were downright barbarous. Adjectives like 'savage' and 'wild' recur intermittently in many accounts of the country. These words were also applied to the Welsh and the crofters of the Scottish Highlands. Some Englishmen believed that there were still living remnants in Ireland of those prehistoric people who had originally inhabited the British Isles.[33] If Englishmen regarded Celtic Irishmen as close to savage, they saw nothing noble about that state. Horace Plunkett met a retired Indian civil servant in county Mayo in August, 1891, who declared that he "could not bear to treat the Irish like white men"; and Plunkett himself once described the people of Erris in Mayo as "little removed from savages."[34] During the Special Commission on Parnellism and crime a number of Irish witnesses came over to London to testify. Max Müller, the noted philologist, wrote to a friend at that time that he would find "plenty of eloquent savages" in town.[35] In an age when the manners and mores of primitive tribes were being studied with greater care, the Irish had to endure comparisons with aboriginal peoples in Africa, the antipodes, and the Orient. Darwin drew a parallel between the Maoris of New Zealand and the Irish peasantry in his chapter on the extinction of races in the *Descent of Man*.[36] In its long campaign against Irish causes the *Times* frequently resorted to abusive adjectives. In 1893, for example, the *Times'* special correspondent, reporting a great Unionist rally in Limerick, contrasted "the solemn and impassioned words" of the assembled Unionists inside the hall with "the wild and savage screams — they were not shouts — which poured from the throats of the tattered rabble without."[37]

There is no more vivid example of the equation which some Englishmen made between apes, savages, and Irishmen than some of the cartoons on Irish affairs in *Punch* and George Cruikshank's illustrations for Maxwell's *History of the Irish Rebellion of 1798*.[38] In both places one may find the Irish Celt portrayed as a creature with half-human and half-simian features. The wild eyes, the prognathous jaw, the ugly mouth and thick lips were designed to emphasize the Irishman's animal instincts and habits. It was not uncommon for English observers to compare Irishmen with the "lowliest" of African tribes, the Hottentots, because they seemed to share so many attributes in common. Who in his right Anglo-Saxonist senses would dream of conferring self-governing institutions on such a people or race?

Another common trait attributed by Englishmen to the Irish Celt was love of violence. Paddy was a fighter by birth and inclination. The word 'Irish' connoted a readiness to fight and one who was 'easily angered'; and 'hooligan' was an epithet derived from a rowdy Irish family which terrorized the residents of south-east London in the 1890's. "The Irishman is never at peace," runs an old Irish saying, "except when he is fighting." English stories about Ireland were filled with allusions to Donnybrook fair and to the generous use of black-thorns or shillelaghs by Mick or Pat. There were countless anecdotes circulating in England about the Irishman's readiness to fight perfect strangers at any time of day or night. Broken heads and bruises abound in the stories of William Carleton, Charles Lever, Michael MacDonagh, and the Halls to name only a few. This love of battle or the shindy was equated in many English minds with social disorder and lawlessness. A writer in the *Edinburgh Review* in 1844 argued that the Irishman's tendency to do violence and to resist the law formed the most prominent and "mischievious" part of Irish character. "All real law," he observed, "is an object of hatred to the mass of the Irish people."[39]

In judging the reality of these stories about the 'fighting Irish' one must bear in mind that the English working classes also had a reputation for violence and brutality. The point here is not that there was no substance to these reports of Irish rowdiness and rioting but

THE IRISH FRANKENSTEIN.

"The baneful and blood-stained Monster ❖ ❖ ❖ yet was it not my Master to the very extent that it was my Creature? ❖ ❖ ❖ Had I not breathed into it my own spirit?" ❖ ❖ ❖ (*Extract from the Works of* C. S. P-RN-LL, M.P.)

OR THE CELTIC CALIBAN

Sir John Tenniel's portrayal in *Punch* of a stereotypical Irish assassin appeared shortly after the murders of Cavendish and Burke in Phoenix Park by Irish Invincibles on May 6, 1882. The artist managed to capture in this picture of "The Irish Frankenstein" the ape-like features, especially the prognathous mouth and jaw and the concave nose, which many English Victorians considered to be distinctive features of Irish Celts. *Punch* described this creature as follows: "Hideous, blood-stained, bestial, ruthless in its rage, implacable in its revengefulness, cynical in its contemptuous challenge of my authority, it seemed another and a fouler *Caliban* in revolt, and successful revolt, against the framer and fosterer of its maleficent existence." *Punch*, 20 May 1882, pp. 234-35.

that some Englishmen believed that all Irishmen loved disorder to the point of anarchy and would never submit voluntarily to the rule of law; hence the conclusion of Peel, Balfour, Long, and other Chief Secretaries that Ireland needed semipermanent coercion or special laws to suppress crime. The Irish Celt was thus condemned by most Anglo-Saxonists for being not only emotionally incontinent but a man of violent passions who indulged in unprovoked attacks on people or executed the vicious orders of secret societies. These traits were part of his nature, they were in his blood, so it was assumed, and no amount of conciliatory legislation could expunge them.

There was another curiously persistent and revealing label attached to the Irish, namely their characterization as a feminine race of people. This theme of Celtic femininity — as opposed to effeminacy — appears repeatedly in Victorian literature along with the implied assumption that the Anglo-Saxons embodied entirely masculine or virile qualities. As we have seen, Renan emphasized the feminine nature of the Celt; and Arnold believed that the sensibility of Celtic nature, "its nervous exaltation," had a feminine quality.[40] Contrasts were drawn between the soft Irish Celts of the south and west of Ireland and the "masculine" Scotch-Irish race of Ulster.[41] On a trip to the Netherlands in 1882, Lady Gregory met an Anglo-Irishman who told her that Europe was divided into two sexes, the male and the female countries. The latter included Italy and the Celtic countries, which had the "soft, pleasing quality and charm of a woman, but no capacity for self-government." It was up to the male countries — England among them — to take the female countries in hand.[42] Another example worth quoting is Sir Horace Plunkett's confession in his diary after a bout of depression: "I am more like a woman than a man, I fear, but that's Irish."[43] The relevance of such attributions to English policy in Ireland lies in the assumed connection between femininity and unfitness for self-government. The habit of assigning sexual gender to various races and nations deserves more rigorous inquiry than can be provided here, but it should be obvious that in a period when demands for female suffrage were being resisted by the overwhelming majority of Conservative and Liberal M.P.'s, when the very idea of female emancipation aroused deep fears among the male members of the population, the assignment of feminine traits of mind to a people like the Irish certainly did not enhance their claim for the political emancipation inherent in Home Rule.

In his classic study of the Negro problem in America, Gunnar Myrdal touched on the parallel between the attitudes of the dominant white male population toward the Negro on the one hand and the "suppressed" white women and children of America on the other.[44] There is an equally striking parallel between the Anglo-Saxonists' image of the Irish Celt in the later nineteenth century and the prevailing attitudes among middle and upper class males in Victorian England toward the two largest dependent and subordinate groups in the country, namely women and children. The parallel is not just one of attitudes but of political policy. In the context of the Irish Question this pattern of thought and action might be expressed as follows: the self-consciously mature and virile Anglo-Saxon had no intention of conferring his sophisticated institutions upon the childlike and feminine Irish Celt.

Needless to say there was nothing modest about Englishmen when it came to discussing their own peculiar genius in political and economic affairs. This self-praise sometimes took the form of an assertion that the Irish could function only within an Anglo-Saxon political and social framework, or that the Irish made good soldiers only when officered by Englishmen.[45] After Parnell and his party had made Home Rule a major issue in British politics, the stereotype of the Irish Celt operated ever more effectively to establish Irish unfitness for self-government. Many of the leaflets printed by the Irish Loyal and Patriotic Union and, later, by the Irish Unionist Alliance stressed the likelihood of civil strife, if not civil war, in a semi-independent Ireland. Irish history was seen by Anglo-Saxonists as nothing more than a series of domestic feuds interrupted by the invasions of civilizing Englishmen. The Irish always had been and always would be hopelessly disunited: "As well might a number of spiders be expected to combine for the purpose of spinning a single web as a band of Irish 'patriots' to pursue one and the same policy," wrote S. C. Hall, who thought he knew Ireland as well as any man.[46] One of the most frequently repeated themes in the 'Irish' jokes and stories that circulated in England concerned the readiness of Irishmen to betray or inform against their best friends.

Some of these Anglo-Saxonist stereotypes cut across party lines

and were entertained by persons of unimpeachable Liberal sentiments on all questions not affecting the Irish. Indeed one might venture further to the left in British political life and still discover good
evidence of anti-Irish sentiments. Take the Webbs for example. When
Sidney and Beatrice Webb were on their working honeymoon in
Dublin in 1892, they wrote to their trusted friend Graham Wallas as
follows:

> We will tell you about Ireland when we come back. The people
> are charming but we detest them, as we should the Hottentots
> — for their very virtues. Home Rule is an absolute necessity *in
> order to depopulate the country of this detestable race.*[47]

So much for a Fabian variation on the Anglo-Saxonist theme.

One of those men of influence whose company the Webbs liked
to cultivate was Arthur Balfour, who came as close as any Anglo-Scot
dared to adopting a doctrinaire Anglo-Saxonist position on the subject of Irish unfitness for self-government. At least in private conver-
sation Balfour could be outspoken about the shortcomings and defects
of the Irish, the French, and other nationalities or races. In 1900, for
example, he told Sir Horace Plunkett over lunch at Number 4 Carlton
Gardens that some nations like the French were not at all suited for
free institutions. "They have all the qualities needed to destroy them,"
Balfour said, and he added that he would not say the same of the
Irish — "publicly."[48] He denied that Irish national sentiment was
either genuine or indigenous. According to Plunkett, who recorded
another talk with him twelve years later, Balfour did not deviate from
this argument. He utterly distrusted "the governing qualities" of the
Irish by which he meant that they lacked "*driving* capacity." He described them as "clever, voluble, ineffective — not trustworthy in
business."[49] James Bryce also had qualms about the readiness of the
Irish for Home Rule in spite of his defense of that policy since 1886.
In 1907, after he had left Ireland for the British Embassy in Washing-
ton, he told Plunkett that Home Rule was no longer practical politics
chiefly because of "the utter unfitness of the people for self-government."[50] Plunkett himself gradually came around to accept Home
Rule as the only possible solution to Irish discontent, but he continued to believe that the character of Irishmen had to be reformed

and strengthened before they could hope to make a success of Home Rule. Character, he insisted, contained the key to the Irish question;[51] and most educated Englishmen would have agreed with him.

The political lesson which many Victorians drew from the prevailing stereotype of the Irish Celt was that the sum of Irish traits, the excess of vices over virtues, rendered the Irish people completely unfit for those ancient Anglo-Saxon liberties, enshrined in the Constitution, which the English people had in their infinite wisdom carefully nurtured and fought to preserve over the centuries. What the Celtic temperament needed was Anglo-Saxon authority and order imposed from above. Paddy was not yet ready for Home Rule because in his ignorant, inexperienced, and unstable hands Anglo-Saxon liberty would degenerate either into anarchy and civil war or into the dictatorship of the Roman Catholic hierarchy and priesthood, presumably at the beck and call of Rome. Such was the political import of the Anglo-Saxonist image of the Irish Celt.

The psychological importance of Paddy can best be explained in terms of the defense mechanism known as projection. The almost mechanical way in which Anglo-Saxonists assigned to Irishmen those very traits which were most deplored or despised among the respectable middle and upper classes in Victorian England leaves little room for doubt that the gentlemen who relied upon this stereotype were merely projecting onto an assumedly inferior group all those emotions which lay buried within themselves and which the English social system encouraged — and at times compelled — them to repress. Projection is one of the most common consequences of repression. When an individual attributes to another individual (or group) those traits and motives which actually threaten his own peace of mind, and when, by so doing, the individual manages to reduce or rationalize away some of his own feelings of guilt, anxiety, or envy, as the case may be, that process is called projection.[52] This psychodynamic process may be found at work in collective as well as individual behavior, and it is especially prevalent where inter-group, inter-ethnic, and international relations are concerned. Some of the most thoroughly documented examples of projection may be found in case studies of anti-Semitism conducted by psychoanalysts and clinical psychologists.[53]

In the context of the Irish Question the striking antithesis between the Anglo-Saxonist's self-image and his image of the Irish Celt, in terms of both physical and mental characteristics, suggest that the holders of these two complementary images were trying to discharge their own anxieties about feelings of violence, indolence, emotional incontinence, and even femininity onto another people who seemed to bear these stigma only too well. Paddy, that feckless, childish, whimsical, and violent Irishman, who so amused and exasperated the later Victorians, served as a convenient scapegoat for the frustrations which arose out of a code of civilized and gentlemanly conduct that regulated the public lives of countless Englishmen. Almost a generation ago Gunnar Myrdal pointed out that the Negro problem in America was "primarily a white man's problem."[54] In much the same way the process of projection made the Irish Question essentially an English question, that is to say, a by-product of the social and emotional pressure under which many middle and upper class Victorians lived and suffered.

CHAPTER V

Anglo-Saxonist Ethnology

In order to understand the ostensibly scientific basis for many of the judgments Englishmen made about Irish character and Celtic behavior it is necessary to examine, however briefly, some of the theories of the Victorian ethnologists and anthropologists who were the acknowledged experts on the subject of man and the varieties of human behavior.[1] If the word race had been used loosely during the first half of the century, it gradually took on a more categorical meaning after the 1850's in the hands of these scientists, some of whom allowed their enthusiasm for this relatively new discipline to dispel the very objectivity and detachment which they proclaimed as the hallmark of their scientific endeavor. Many of those who joined the new ethnological and anthropological societies in England in the 1860's and 1870's were newcomers to this field, with no special skills at their command to distinguish them from ancient historians and archaeologists, and with the kind of ethnocentric prejudices that made their lectures and published work resemble at times polemics couched in the current scientific language of the day. There were, of course, some notable exceptions to this pattern, among them men like James Prichard, E. B. Tylor, the so-called 'father' of British anthropology, and Sir John Lubbock, whose intellectual and personal qualities enabled them to produce more objective work in this burgeoning field.[2] But the differences in ethnocentrism between the few eminent men at the top and the many rank and file members of these societies were those of degree rather than kind. Few ethnologists in England in these decades were capable of writing about Irish Celts, American Negroes, and African Hottentots, for example, with any degree of detachment; and the very choice of such subjects for anthropological investigation affords some indication of the present mindedness and political sensitivity of some of these scientists of society, culture, and race.

It was from this group of energetic and dedicated ethnologists and anthropologists that much of the scientific evidence was derived which was used to condemn Irish Celts to various stages of inferiority. In general the most blatant examples of Anglo-Saxonist ethnology, where Irishmen and Negroes as well as comparisons between the two were involved, came from those men whose approach was primarily physiological and anatomical. They were the heirs apparent of such continental past masters of comparative anatomy, craniology, and physiognomy as Baron Cuvier, Johann Blumenbach, Pieter Camper, L. A. D. Quetelet, and Anders Retzius. The Anglo-Saxonist ethnologists of Victorian England had their analogues in America too, where ethnocentrism was rife in the work of anthropologists like G. R. Gliddon, J. C. Nott, and S. G. Morton, all of whom saw intimate and vital connections between cranial size, intelligence, national character, and race.[3]

In England the 1860's and 1870's were decades of relatively rapid growth both in the number of those who were practicing some form of ethnology and those who were reading and discussing the results of that research. It is by no means easy to distinguish between ethnology and anthropology in Victorian England because the terms were often used in practice as synonymous, and as a result of the controversies which raged over questions of substance, methodology, and, last but not least, personality, a man might call himself an anthropologist simply because he refused to belong to the Ethnological Society of London. T. H. Huxley once defined ethnology as the science which "determines the distinctive characters of the persistent modifications of mankind, which ascertains the distribution of those modifications in present and past times, and seeks to discover the cause or conditions of existence, both of the modifications and their distribution." And he then proceeded to describe ethnology as a branch of anthropology — "the great science which unravels the complexities of human structure; traces out the relations of man to other animals; studies all that is especially human in the mode in which man's complex functions are performed; and searches after the conditions which have determined his presence in the world." Now Huxley was anxious to demonstrate that anthropology was a subsection of zoology which in turn was a subdivision of the queen of the sciences, biology, "the science of life."[4] But in practice the members of the Anthropological and Ethnological Societies did not make such fine distinctions between the researches carried out under the auspices or with the blessing of these two organizations. Definitions of ethnology in this period ranged from the handmaiden or tool of the philologist and archaeologist to "the science of blood, or races of mankind resulting from genealogical descent."[5] The point is that race thinking and assumptions about the permanence of racial characteristics suffused the researches of these ethnologists and anthropologists, who were anxious to expose what they called the Christian and liberal superstitions about mankind which misled so many of their contemporaries. The elaborate definition of their 'new' science with which some of these men armed themselves did not prevent much of their work from being concerned with the origins, varieties, and inequalities of the races of man.

The relevance of British ethnology and anthropology to the Irish Question lies in the ingenious attempts of certain scientific students of race to explain the origins of the modern British people by identifying and differentiating the various racial components of the population, from Britons, Saxons, Celts, and Picts to Danes and Normans, on the basis of their alleged physical and mental characteristics. The researches of these ethnologists were sustained by the conviction that race rather than environment or climate determined human behavior, and it was assumed that membership in any race could be ascertained by merely examining the skull or head shape, the color of hair and eyes, the pigmentation, the degree of prognathism or orthognathism, and the stature and carriage of the specimen in question. Calipers, cephalic indexes, color charts to determine the shade of hair and eye, facial angles, and other elaborate devices made up the methodological tool bag of these taxonomists of the human species. Encouraged by the renewed interest in the origins of all organic life, much of which stemmed from the publication of Darwin's and Wallace's theories about evolution, some of these ethnologists set to work to discover just what the origins of the modern British people were and why the English and the Irish seemed to behave in such different ways. Invariably blind to the ethnocentrism which lurked within their minds, these scientists played their part in aggravating the scepticism of many English legislators and public men about the capacity of the Irish Celt to manage his own affairs.

The unflattering image of Irishmen which was constructed by some of these ethnologists may be seen to best or worst advantage in the pages of the *Anthropological Review* and the *Journal of the Ethnological Society*. These two journals constitute a rich source of anti-Irish propaganda in the 1860's, and the similarities between the stereotype of Irish behavior to be found there and the popular version of Paddy are too close to be coincidental. As one might expect of men who categorized Irishmen and Negroes according to assumed differences of race and character, the more prejudiced of these ethnologists had no use for the doctrine of the rights of man and racial equality. James Hunt, that pugnacious and domineering man who played the leading role in founding the Anthropological Society of London in 1863 as a rival to the Ethnological Society, once scolded John Bright for having said in a speech that whatever was defective in the Irish people was the result of the conditions to which they had been subjected in the past rather than of race. The truth was just the reverse. All the evidence indicated, at least to Hunt, that men were wholly unequal, and that some races could never be civilized; and it was the duty of anthropologists not only to find out why but to point up the fallacious arguments of "closet philosophers" like John Stuart Mill and men suffering from the "religious mania."[6]

Just as doctrinaire as Hunt on the subject of racial inequality was Robert Knox, the famous, or rather notorious, anatomist who had bought a number of cadavers from Burke and Hare — those two sinister Irish Celts — in the 1820's. Knox was a popular lecturer on the physiological aspects of race, and his best known work, *The Races of Man*, appeared in 1850. He had a well deserved reputation for pungent epigrams and heavy irony at the expense of those who disagreed with him; and he made his position clear at the outset of his book by declaring: "With me race, or hereditary descent, is everything; it stamps the man." Knox was a dogmatic racial purist who insisted that nature so abhorred hybrid races that they could not survive for any length of time. The mixture of Celt and Saxon produced a people of "uncertain character" who soon died out or returned to the purer races. Convinced that conflict dominated the relations of races in the world, Knox argued that Saxon and Celt were mutually and inherently antagonistic. Since time immemorial the Saxon had been everywhere the same in character: "nature's democrat — the respecter of law when the law is made *by himself.*" The Saxon was "thoughtful, plodding, industrious." He loved order, punctuality, good business methods, and cleanliness. Unlike the Celt he did not object to working for profit; and no race surpassed him in self-confidence or in the desire to accumulate wealth.[7] The prospect of successful cross-breeding between Irish Celts and English Saxons was out of the question in Knox's view. Seven hundred years of English occupation of Ireland had not brought such an amalgamation any nearer to achievement. The Celt himself had little to recommend him:

> The Celt does not understand what we Saxons mean by independence; he understands a military leader, a faction fight, a fortified camp. . . . I appeal to the Saxon men of all countries whether I am right or not in my estimate of the Celtic character. Furious fanaticism; a love of war and disorder; a hatred for order and patient industry; no accumulative habits; restless, treacherous, uncertain: look at Ireland. . . . As a Saxon, I abhor all dynasties, monarchies and bayonet governments, but this latter seems to be the only one suitable for the Celtic man.[8]

Knox was thus convinced that Celts, whether in France or Ireland, simply did not know the meaning of rational liberty and could not be entrusted with freedom. Whereas the Celts were natural revolutionaries, the Saxons were natural reformers. Civilized man could not sink lower than he had done in the west of Ireland; and the Irishman posed a more serious threat to Anglo-Saxon social order and political stability than any other kind of Celt.

Among the ethnologists who preferred more quantitative methods to purely descriptive studies of races was D. Mackintosh who relied almost entirely on visual observation in making his distinctions among Saxon, Celtic, and Gaelic types. He differentiated the Celts of Wales from the Gaels of southwestern England and Ireland on the basis of shape and size of head, nose, mouth, and jaw and color of eyes and hair. According to Mackintosh the Gael was marked by his bulging jaw and lower part of face, retreating chin and forehead, large mouth and thick lips, great distance between nose and mouth, upturned nose, prominent cheekbones, sunken eyes, projecting eyebrows, narrow, elongated skull and protruding ears. His picture of Gaelic mental characteristics was equally revealing:

> Quick in perception, but deficient in depth of reasoning power; headstrong and excitable; tendency to oppose; strong in love and hate; at one time lively, soon after sad, vivid in imagination; extremely social, with a propensity for crowding together; forward and self-confident; deficient in application to deep study, but possessed of great concentration in monotonous or purely mechanical occupations, such as hop-picking, reaping, weaving etc.; want of prudence and foresight; antipathy to sea-faring pursuits . . . veneration for authority.[9]

Mackintosh followed this portrait of the Gael with an almost lyrical description of the physical and mental characteristics of the Saxon. His features were extremely regular: mouth well formed, chin neither prominent nor receding, nose straight, eyes prominent, ears flat, hair light brown, chest and shoulders of moderate breadth. In mentality the Saxon stood for moderation in all things. His character was "simple, truthful, straightforward, and honest . . . determined, but not self-willed; self-reliant yet humble; peaceable, orderly, unexcitable, unambitious, and free from extravagance."[10] This racial narcissism did not stop here. As if Saxon virtues were not enough, Mackintosh went on to praise the enviable attributes of a so-called Anglian type. Taken together, as Mackintosh no doubt intended, these two idealized types of Saxon and Angle, when seasoned with certain Danish virtues, added up to the very model of a modern Anglo-Saxon. In a political, if not scientific sense, British ethnology had come of age.

One of the most influential students of race in Britain after 1860 was Dr. John Beddoe, a Bristol physician and prolific ethnologist.[11] Beddoe was something of a pioneer in the use of quantitative methods in the field of ethnology. Perhaps his most famous work, *The Races of Britain,* published in 1885, derived from an essay which had won first prize at the national Eisteddfod in 1868. Beddoe spent the next fifteen years refining and applying his "numerical and inductive method" to the ethnology of both Britain and Western Europe. His work was notable for its attempt to classify races by color of hair and eyes as well as by stature and physiognomy; and his work on color led him to invent the "index of nigrescence," that exotic formula designed to identify the various racial components of a given people.[12] Beddoe carried much further than Mackintosh the technique of quantifying the visual observations he made in the field or on the main streets of towns and cities. Like most of his scientific colleagues he was a firm believer in the dissimilarity of Saxon and Celt. In 1867 he had written that he did not understand the Irish — perhaps because he had too much Saxon blood in him; but he was absolutely sure that an Irishman of "totally pure blood" differed completely from a "typical Englishman" both in physical and mental characteristics. Although Beddoe denied that the Irish were an innately inferior race to the Saxons, he believed that racial differences explained the failure of the English to govern Ireland.[13] The importance of Beddoe's work was not confined to the antithesis which he drew between Celt or Gael and Anglo-Saxon. Beddoe contended that in Ireland one could still find the residual survivals of a primitive people who had certain affinities with Cro-Magnon or "Africanoid" man.[14] His index of nigrescence served to prove that the Irish were darker than the people of eastern and central England and that they were closer in physical type to the aborigines of the British Isles who in turn had traces of Negro ancestry in their appearance. Relying on his "instinct" and on a recent survey of Cambridge undergraduates which established a strong correlation between those who took First Class degrees and those who had light hair and blue eyes,[15] Beddoe managed to add to the already derogatory image of the Irish Celt compiled by his fellow ethnologists a distinctive form of color prejudice. Just how white-skinned were Irishmen? Who were the so-called 'black Irish,' and where did they come from? How close was a prognathous and nigrescent Celt to a Negro? Such questions were implicit and at times explicit in Beddoes' work; and the implicit answer was that not all men in the British Isles were equally white or equal.

Such examples as these serve to make some Victorian anthropologists look much more like apologists for an alleged Anglo-Saxon civilization and physique. But fortunately for the future of British anthropology the attitudes of men like Hunt and Knox dominated a few disciples rather than the discipline itself, and by the end of the century there were far fewer ethnologists who believed that the Celt was as incapable of changing his habits as the leopard his spots or the Ethiopian his skin.[16]

CHAPTER VI

Anglo-Saxonist Historiography

Apart from the ethnologists and anthropologists, the Victorians who gave the greatest impetus to the dichotomy of Saxon and Celt were some of the most eminent historians in the country. These men were better placed than ethnologists to promote Anglo-Saxonist doctrines, especially because they wrote regularly for the established periodicals with which educated Englishmen and women satisfied their intellectual appetites. Their major works, moreover, reached a far larger audience and were more often reviewed and discussed than were those of men like Knox or Beddoe. Few of the leading historians in the second half of the century shunned publicity, and most of them relished their participation in public controversies ranging from the Governor Eyre dispute to the American Civil War, the Eastern Question, and Irish Home Rule. Such issues were almost as likely to drive these politicized historians into print as did their quest for the origins of English political stability and economic prosperity in the remote or recent past. Since many of the parliamentarians who voted on the Home Rule bills of 1886 and 1893 owed what history they knew to the works of men like Lord Macaulay, Edward Freeman, John R. Green, James A. Froude, and Bishop Stubbs, it is important to know what these historians were thinking and writing about the development of English political liberties in general and the nature of Irish Celts in patricular. As we will see, most of these historians not only shared the prevalent stereotype of Paddy, but they did much, whether unwittingly or not, to harden that image of the Irish Celt in their lectures and published works.

The period from 1850 to the early 1890's was a formative one in

English historiography, no matter how ephemeral some of the works written in those years turned out to be. Constitutional, legal, and institutional history flourished as never before, and medievalists like Freeman, Stubbs, and Green enjoyed a vogue that was marked by the plaudits of scholars on the Continent and in America as well as by the material rewards emanating from their publishers.[1] The leading historians of this period combined distinctive literary talents with more exacting standards of textual criticism to produce such classic works as Stubbs' *Constitutional History* and Lecky's *History of England in the Eighteenth Century*. The greater reliance of these historians on new primary sources did not immunize them, however, against the infectious disease of Anglo-Saxonism. Almost all the major English medieval and modern historians in this era, with the exception of Sir Francis Palgrave, S. R. Gardiner, and, to some extent, Lecky, were staunch Anglo-Saxonists who were prepared to argue that the English people really did possess a unique genius for good government and for ordering their domestic and imperial affairs with success.

However risky it may be to generalize about historians as different in personality as Freeman, Green, Stubbs, and Froude, all these men were in fundamental agreement about the supreme virtues of the English Constitution, as it had evolved from Anglo-Saxon times, and they attributed the proverbial stability of English political institutions to the long and courageous devotion of the Anglo-Saxon people to an ideal of personal and civil liberty — a devotion which had survived such traumatic experiences as the Norman Conquest and the civil wars of the seventeenth century. Zealously pursuing their researches into pre-Norman England as well as into the political problems of succeeding centuries, these historians created an historical orthodoxy that reached the height of its influence in the third quarter of the century. The Anglo-Saxonist historians derived some of their precedents from the Gothicists of an earlier period, but they owed most of their faith in the science of history to such formidable German historians as Ranke, Mommsen, Waitz, and Jacob Grimm,[2] and for their belief in the organic growth of the embryonic liberties of Anglo-Saxons into the full grown, mature, and, indeed, masculine institutions of modern Britain they were more indebted than they realized to the evolutionary theories of Darwin, Wallace, Huxley,

Spencer, Benjamin Kidd, Francis Galton, and Karl Pearson. These ethnocentric historians may be called a school with no formal curriculum and no predominant methodology. The Anglo-Saxonism of its members was sufficiently ecumenical to include both Freeman and Froude whose historiographical feuding delighted many a reader of the *Saturday Review*.

Perhaps the best known publicist of Anglo-Saxonism in its pre-racialist phase was Sharon Turner, whose *History of the Anglo-Saxons* was published between 1799 and 1805. This sympathetic account of the origins, manners, migrations, and political activities of the Anglo-Saxons so pleased the reading public that his volumes reached their seventh edition in 1852. Turner's work was distinguished by a flattering, full-length portrait of Alfred the Great and by a number of tributes paid to the self-governing capacity of the Anglo-Saxons. His book brimmed over with approval of the enduring quality of 'Anglo-Saxon genius.' In a passage which marked him as the first of the nineteenth-century Anglo-Saxonist historians Turner wrote:

> Yet from such ancestors a nation has, in the course of twelve centuries been formed, which, inferior to none in every moral and intellectual merit, is superior to every other in the love and possession of useful liberty: a nation which cultivates with equal success the elegancies of art, the ingenious labours of industry, the energies of war, the researches of science, and the richest productions of genius.[3]

Turner thus worked hard to shorten the cultural gap between the reigns of Alfred the Great and George III, and the bridge which he built between these two epochs out of such traditional materials as pride in Parliament and common law turned out to be strong enough to sustain many a reader for several generations.

As in so many other aspects of English attitudes towards Ireland, there are striking continuities in the ways English historians tended to look at the Irish people. As Geoffrey Keating, the notable seventeenth century Irish historian wrote: "If, indeed it be that the soil is commended by every historian who writes on Ireland, the race is dispraised by every new foreign historian who writes about it. . . ."[4] The same might have been said about English historians in the 1870's, except that these men believed that they had scientific proof of the inferiority of Irish Celts. Lord Macaulay was not a full-blooded Anglo-Saxonist, but in his teleological approach to the Glorious Revolution and its Williamite settlement one may find indications of a Whiggish ethnocentrism, especially where the Irish were concerned. Take for example the following passage from *The History of England*:

> The Irish, on the other hand, were distinguished by qualities which tend to make men interesting rather than prosperous. They were an ardent and impetuous race, easily moved to tears or to laughter, to fury or to love. Alone among the nations of Northern Europe they had the susceptibility, the vivacity, the natural turn for acting and rhetoric which are indigenous on the shores of the Mediterranean Sea. In mental cultivation Scotland had an indisputable superiority.[5]

Anglo-Saxonist historiography did not really reach maturity until the theory of the mark had been firmly transplanted from German universities like Göttingen and Berlin to London, Oxford, and Cambridge. The man who did most to transplant the mark was John Mitchell Kemble, who had studied at Göttingen under Jacob Grimm in the early 1830's and who published his major work, *The Saxons in England,* in 1849.[6] Kemble was convinced that the so-called mark had evolved through at least three stages and that Parliament itself was a natural culmination of this historical process. The mark was first held to be a boundary between two fields, two or more villages, or two or more districts. It then became a tract of common land, access to which was free for the members of the surrounding communities which recognized the sovereignty of the law protecting the mark. At length it turned into the "free village community" itself, in which the laws of property and the relations between and among the mark-men were based on a common fund of custom, usage, and law. The mark meant many things to its champions in the middle decades of the nineteenth century, but whether it was construed as a small tract of forest lying between two villages or a body of law guaranteeing the liberties of all good Saxon freemen, the apostles of this theory were agreed that the mark was a peculiarly German, Teutonic, Saxon, or Anglo-Saxon institution, quite foreign to the experience of less sophisticated peoples like the Celts.[7]

The mark theory dominated English medieval studies, at least in

Oxford, for over a generation, that is to say from the 1850's to 1890 or thereabouts, and its appeal to historians was remarkable in view of the scanty documentation on which it rested. The sources of the theory lay deep in the minds of those romantic German scholars in the French revolutionary era who were determined to make the study of the past into a science. Among the men who elaborated this powerful mythology about the special development of Teutonic institutions in the pagan past were F. K. von Savigny, Jacob Grimm, August Schlegel, Georg Waitz, and, above all, Georg L. von Maurer and his son, Konrad von Maurer.[8] In England the mark was taken up with enthusiasm by Kemble, Freeman, Stubbs, and Sir Henry Maine. The mark theory not only imbued Anglo-Saxonist historiography with a distinctly ethnic and at times racialist aura owing to the German or Saxon content of this transplantation, but it reinforced the beliefs of many well educated Englishmen that their own ancient liberties were specifically designed by and intended for Anglo-Saxons only and were certainly not suitable for Celts. The mark theory caught on fast in Oxford, especially after the appointments of Stubbs and Freeman as Regius Professors of Modern History, and it appealed to most of the young history dons who were searching for some mechanism that would explain why the fittest institutions in Western Europe, indeed in the world, had survived first and foremost in England. The theory proved highly resistant to criticism, and it withstood for a time the frontal attack of Fustel de Coulanges in the 1880's and the flank attacks of Vinogradoff in England and Charles M. Andrews in America in the early 1890's.[9] Not until Maitland had arrived on the medievalist scene did the mark begin to fade away from English historical circles.

In his efforts to trace the genius of English political and social institutions back to the earliest known inhabitants of 'Sleswick' and 'Heiligisland', John Kemble turned to the mark which the Saxon invaders had brought with them to Britain. These Anglo-Saxon settlers saw to it, according to Kemble, that the mark blossomed into a legal and constitutional network of rights and privileges, sanctified by custom and time immemorial, which not only enshrined the rights of private as well as communal property, but helped to preserve the peace between and among the members of a tribe or nation. Kemble's work on the Saxons in England might also be described as Whiggish ethnocentrism: "The Englishman," he wrote, "has inherited the noblest portion of his being from the Anglo-Saxons. In spite of every influence we bear a marvellous resemblance to our forefathers."[10] Few English readers could resist this highly digestible pabulum either in the 1850's or for decades thereafter.

Kemble's Anglo-Saxonism was calm and cautious in comparison with that of Edward Augustus Freeman, who carried the mark forward with all the vigor and aggressiveness of an academic crusader. Judged by the force of his personality and the dogmatism of his mind, Freeman was the mightiest Anglo-Saxonist of them all. With pugnacity, erudition, and a passion for blending politics and history to the point where they became inseparable, Freeman took up where Kemble left off in the search for the German roots of English civil liberties. Born in 1823 of a modest landowning family in Staffordshire, Freeman was blessed with a name which epitomized his mission as an historian. With seemingly inexhaustible energy and enthusiasm he spent most of his adult life in seeking the origins of *liber homo* in Western Europe and in investigating the social and political structure in which the Anglo-Saxon freeman of the eighth or ninth century had developed into the modern, enlightened Englishman of the 1860's. Freeman found his archetype of the free man among those Saxon adventurers who had carried their sacred institutions from German forests into Britain. Freeman was not only a champion of Anglo-Saxonism but an exponent of comparative history who insisted that the comparison of political and social organizations in the past offered the best way to understand the past as well as the present and possibly even the future.

In the spring of 1873 Freeman delivered a series of lectures in London, which were published under the title *Comparative Politics,* in which he utilized some of the techniques of comparative history in order to advance the Anglo-Saxonist thesis. Although he showed some indebtedness to the work of F. Max Müller, Sir Francis Palgrave, and Sir Henry Maine, Freeman relied mainly on his own resources in arguing that the three greatest branches of the great Aryan race — the Greeks, the Romans, and the Teutons — were responsible for the civilizing of Europe and the new world. In the institutions and languages of Western Europe he detected a fundamental unity and continuity of development based on common kinship. According to Freeman the Greeks, Romans, and Teutons had each in their day been entrusted with a mission to be "the rulers and the teachers of the world"; and the English people were the "truest representatives" of the Teutonic race because, of all the nations of Europe, England alone could boast that its institutions descended in an unbroken line from "primitive Teutonic stock." Firm in the conviction that the English Parliament could be traced directly back at least to the meeting of the witan of Wessex that had confirmed Alfred's laws, Freeman argued that the mark or *gemeine* was proof of the Teutonic origins of English polity, and he went on to declare that the Celtic race in France had played a formidable part in European history only by adopting Teutonic forms and by speaking one of the many Roman dialects. After comparing the political institutions of the Greeks, Romans, and Teutons, he concluded that if English political development had been slower and less brilliant than that of the Greeks and Romans, it had also been more "sure" and permanent. To the Teutons belonged the credit of fostering the idea of the nation state as opposed to the city state; and to English or Anglo-Saxon culture Freeman attributed all that was most worth preserving and emulating in the affairs of civilized man.[11]

A strong current of Anglo-Saxonism ran through almost all of Freeman's writings and lectures. In 1849, for example, he reviewed Kemble's *Saxons in England* in the *Guardian*, and attributed England's escape from the revolutions that had "tottered thrones and convulsed societies" on the Continent to the free and stable institutions which the modern English people had inherited from their "Teutonic forefathers."[12] For Freeman this Anglo-Saxon or Teutonic inheritance served as a form of vaccination against dangerous political diseases from Paris or Berlin. Like the anthropologist Hunt, Freeman was a man of passionate likes and dislikes. He had no love for the French, whom he accused of vainglory, conceit, and Napoleonic yearnings; he preferred the sturdy Normans to the effete Parisians; and he felt quite at home in Switzerland where he once witnessed the summoning of the *Landesgemeinde* or representative assembly of the canton — a ceremony that stirred his Anglo-Saxonist soul to the very depths.[13]

While Freeman might deal in superlatives in discussing the political institutions of the free Swiss and the ancient free Saxons, the sight of Irishmen seemed to bring out the worst in him. There was nothing mild about his Anglo-Saxonist reactions to Irish Celts, or Negroes for that matter, when he wrote to a friend from New Haven, Connecticut, in December, 1881:

> This would be a grand land if only every Irishman would kill a negro, and be hanged for it. I find this sentiment generally approved — sometimes with the qualification that they want Irish and negroes for servants, not being able to get any other. This looks like the ancient human weakness of craving for a subject race.[14]

For all his polemical reviews, indiscreet *obiter dicta,* and heavy-handed assaults on the work of Froude, and no doubt because of them, Freeman was taken seriously by many of his contemporaries, and on his visit to America in 1881-82 he proved his effectiveness as a preacher of the Anglo-Saxonist creed. Using much the same language and emotional appeal to Anglo-Saxon kinship as had appeared in Dilke's *Greater Britain,* he declared that Americans and Englishmen were not strangers or aliens to one another but bearers of the same culture and sharers of the same blood. At Johns Hopkins University he bestowed his blessing upon the Anglo-Saxonist work of Herbert Baxter Adams, and his visit there was commemorated by a portrait of the historian along with his favorite epigram, borrowed from Seeley: "History is past politics, politics are present history." Freeman returned to England from his American trip in April, 1882, on board the S.S. *Germanic,* sailing from New York.[15]

As his obituary in the *Manchester Guardian* stated, Freeman "gloried in the Germanic origin of the English nation." He was an ethnocentric purist who complained of the corruption of the English language by Latin and Roman elements. James Bryce, who knew him from their Oxford association, explained that Freeman welcomed the plan to remove the Irish members from Westminister in 1886 because he was "intensely English and Teutonic, and wished the Celts to be left to settle their own affairs in their own island, as they had done centuries ago."[16] Freeman himself had put this sentiment more bluntly, when he wrote to Bryce during the debate on the first Home Rule bill: "I do hope Gladstone will stick firm to shutting out the Paddies from Westminster. It is one of the pillars of the whole thing."[17]

Working in an altogether different key — less belligerent, highly Tory, and more restrained — and writing a rich, episcopal prose, Bishop Stubbs was also an Anglo-Saxonist who warmly embraced the idea of the mark as put forth by Kemble and G. L. von Maurer. Although he succumbed to the "science of Teutonic origins," as it was being practiced in Germany, Stubbs was too acute an historian to allow his theory to dominate his thought at the expense of enduring insights as Freeman had done. Stubbs was a firm believer in national character, but he took care to point out that English character was as much a consequence as a cause of English history. At the outset of the *Constitutional History* he unfurled his Anglo-Saxonist banner:

> The English are not aboriginal. . . . They are a people of German descent in the main constituents of blood, character, and language, but most especially, in connexion with our subject, in the possession of the elements of primitive German civilisation and the common germs of German institutions. This descent is not a matter of inference. It is a recorded fact of history which these characteristics bear out to the fullest degree of certainty.[18]

Stubbs' comments on the Irish people were not often published; but one at least is worth quoting as an indication of where his sympathies lay:

> Things in general are very flat here: Egypt only in a slight degree drawing men's thoughts away from Ireland. If the Jews are on their way back to Palestine, could not the Irish be prevailed on *antiquam exquirer matrem* and emigrate in search of Scota, Pharoah's daughter?[19]

Closely associated with Freeman and Stubbs both in friendship and historiography was John Richard Green, who began his researches into the English past with something less than affection for Celts, possibly because some Welsh students had annoyed him while he was an undergraduate at Jesus College, Oxford. A brief tour through Wales convinced him about the "Ishmaelitish character" of the Celtic race, but on his first trip to Ireland he gained such a favorable impression of Irish hospitality that he was moved to write a bit of dubious doggerel about the "land of the Paddies."[20] Green's Anglo-Saxonism, more tepid than that of Freeman, found an outlet in his *Short History of the English People,* wherein the antithesis of Celt and Teuton emerges clearly. "In the Celtic love of woman," he declared, "there is little of the Teutonic depth and earnestness . . . the sensibility of the Celtic temper . . . is tempered by a passionate melancholy that expresses itself in revolt against the impossible." For Green the Celts were "fickle" and deficient in powers of organization, in marked contrast to the Germans who possessed a "grandeur, depth, and fervour of tone," and as we have seen, he believed that English liberties had been first nurtured by Engles and Jutes in Schleswig before they were brought by these sturdy, honest folk to England.[21] Like Freeman, Green became an early convert to Irish Home Rule, and both men are good examples of the fact that Anglo-Saxonism did not always bolster the cause of imperial consolidation and expansion. Just as there were a few Conservative Home Rulers in England in the 1880's, so too there were some Anglo-Saxonist Liberals who stuck to Gladstone through thick and thin. And in Freeman's case — Green having died in 1883, before the advent of the first Home Rule Bill — his extreme veneration for pure Anglo-Saxon institutions provided all the more reason for his wanting to see the disruptive Irish Celtic element purged from Westminster. Whatever their intentions, the Anglo-Saxonist content of Freeman's and Green's historical writings made effective propaganda for the Unionist cause.

In contrast to the Home Rule sympathies of Freeman and Green, there was another Oxford scholar, the noted jurist Albert Venn Dicey, who was convinced that the Irish were unfit to govern themselves. Dicey was one of Bryce's closest friends, and yet he opposed him vigorously over the question of Home Rule. He accepted as a fact of life that the civilized and uncivilized races of man were locked in perpetual and often deadly conflict; he believed in the existence of a "more or less permanent national character"; and he predicted that a native Irish government would inevitably pass from a state of anarchy to a French or authoritarian type of regime.[22] For such reasons Dicey became one of the Unionist party's leading advocates against Home Rule.

An equally outspoken critic of Irish nationalism was Goldwin Smith, the once radical essayist, historian, and controversialist whose low estimate of Celtic character colored not only his politics but such books as *Irish History and Irish Character* (1861) and the more topical *Irish History and the Irish Question* (1905). The first of these works was rife with the idea of struggle between Saxon and Celt, and almost every page added some new contrast to this racial antithesis. Although Smith believed that race was the most important physical influence affecting the character and destiny of nations, he did concede that education could do much to transform character and assimilate one race to another. In his opinion the clannish Celt preferred subservience to a king or despot to freedom. The Teuton, on the other hand, was a constitutionalist who loved laws, parliaments, and free institutions. Loyalty was the chief virtue of Irish political character, the great defect of which was "want of independence and of that strong sense of right by which law and personal liberty are upheld."[23]

While Oxford audiences were being exposed to Anglo-Saxonist versions of the mark theory, Cambridge undergraduates were flocking to the lectures of Charles Kingsley, whose worship of all things Saxon and English suffused his outlook on the past. Whatever his defects as an historian, Kingsley was a superb story teller. He enthralled his audiences with tales of intensely English heroes who served as models for some of the mighty heroes in *Hereward the Wake* and other novels. The idea of profound racial conflict ran through his famous lectures, which were published under the title, *The Roman and the Teuton*.[24] Some sense of Kingsley's attitudes toward the Irish may be gained from the letter he wrote to his wife in July, 1860, during a brief sojourn in Ireland:

> But I am haunted by the human chimpanzees I saw along that hundred miles of horrible country. I don't believe they are our fault. I believe there are not only many more of them than of old, but that they are happier, better, more comfortably fed and lodged under our rule than they ever were. But to see white chimpanzees is dreadful; if they were black, one would not feel it so much, but their skins, except where tanned by exposure, are as white as ours.[25]

Like Negroid analogy, like simian simile . . . .

There was one English historian who did not need to rely upon the mark theory in order to sustain his militant Anglo-Saxonism. More

than any of his fellow historians James Anthony Froude exemplified
the Celtophobia which underlay so much of the Unionist campaign
against Home Rule as well as the writing of Irish history in England.[26]
Froude's researches into that history were animated by his desire to
discover why it was that the Irish people had achieved so little of
value in comparison with their English neighbors and rulers. As in
the case of so many of his contemporaries, Froude found the answer
he wanted in race and national character. One of the curious things
about Froude is that he had spent more time in Ireland than any
other English historian of his day. On his first trip to that country in
1840 the contrast between the serenity of Anglo-Irish civilization and
the misery of Celtic Ireland had fascinated him, and he returned to
Ireland in 1845, 1848, and again in the years 1867 to 1870 when he
spent the summers writing in a house rented from Lord Lansdowne
at Derreen. His love of the country itself remained undimmed by the
famine and by the lowly estimate he had formed of Irish character.

It would be an understatement to call Froude's portrait of Paddy
unflattering. In his autobiographical fragment he once described the
Irish as "the most superstitious, the most imaginative and inflamma-
ble people in Europe." On a drive from Bandon to Killarney in 1845
he had encountered people who seemed "more like tribes of squalid
apes than human beings." In Catholic Ireland, he wrote, nothing
thrived except the Church; the truth was that an "evil genius" hung
over the country.[27] Froude never denied the great kindness and
charm of the Irish people, and he had rather a soft spot for the Paddies. Unfortunately they suffered from incurable faults in their political and social organization and they required the presence of a
superior race in order to keep them up to the mark. Such prejudices
about Celtic Ireland not only informed his study of *The English in
Ireland* but they inspired his novel, the *Two Chiefs of Dunboy*,
wherein the theme of racial conflict between Saxon and Celt predomi-
nates.[28] Froude embodied that struggle in the persons of Colonel
Goring, the English evangelical and improving landlord — a composite figure resembling both Cromwell and Joseph Chamberlain —
and Morty Sullivan, patterned on many an Irish rebel leader, fiercely
proud, daring and desperate. Froude depicted the Irish people as
being "unstable as water," and as synonymous with anarchy and
unbridled passion, whereas the English stood for order and self-

control.[29] Froude's tale of violent conflict between two races and cultures ended, not surprisingly, with the deaths of both heroes, as though their demise symbolized the fatal collision of the two islands.

In his historical works Froude played on the theme of a prolonged struggle between two races for ascendancy in Ireland; the mightier English had been unable to subdue the weaker Irish for centuries largely because they had misunderstood Irish character. What the Irish respected was brute force and steady, unyielding government. The antithesis of Protestant Saxon and Catholic Celt runs throughout the *History of England*. According to Froude, the "fatal fascination" of the Anglo-Norman conquerors with the Irish spirit had caused most of the trouble in Ireland; and he described that spirit as "an impatience of control, a deliberate preference for disorder, a determination in each individual man to go his own way, whether it was a good way or a bad, and a reckless hatred of industry." Only one form of government could ever have succeeded in Ireland and that was an "efficient military despotism," because the "wild Irish" understood only force.[30] It is hardly necessary to add that Froude prescribed the same remedy for Irish troubles in the 1880's.

The apologist of the Protestant reformation and the English occupation of Ireland soon turned to a full-length study of Anglo-Irish relations in the eighteenth century, and in 1872 the first volume of *The English in Ireland* appeared. Froude dedicated this important work to that stern champion of Anglo-Irish culture, Sir Garnet Wolseley, whom he called "the most distinguished living representative of the English in Ireland." This highly ethnocentric study emphasized the inability of the Irish to show the courage and resolution of the Scottish people and the inability of the English to conciliate the Irish or to prevent them from rebelling. Mindful of the intimate connection between might and right, as befitted the leading disciple of Carlyle, Froude ventured to declare that had the Irish been successful in their struggle for freedom, they would then have acquired the qualities which would have made them worthy of that freedom.[31]

Like Dilke, Froude noted a similarity between the Irish and Asians: both had to be governed with firmness, otherwise they would begin to cut throats. Whereas an Englishman would revolt against any kind of despotism, an Irishman was "instinctively loyal to an authority which is not afraid to assert itself. He respects courage; he despises cowardice. Rule him resolutely, and he will not rebel; rule him justly and he will follow you to the world's end."[32] Only a few references to Parnellism needed to be added to this passage to make it read like an excerpt from a Unionist speech or pamphlet in the 1880's or 1890's. Even before the completion of this book in 1874, the young Anglo-Irish historian William Lecky had set to work to demolish the foundations of Froude's thesis in two long reviews in *Macmillan's Magazine* in which he accused the author of trying to defame the Irish people by means of distorted evidence and extreme partiality.[33]

The various scathing reviews which *The English in Ireland* provoked did little to chasten Froude; and in 1879 he wrote a long and unrepentant article in the *North American Review,* entitled "Romanism and the Irish Race," which was nothing more than a frontal assault on the Roman Catholic Church in America as well as on the hordes of Irishmen who made that Church such a menace to Anglo-Saxon and Protestant civilization. Froude argued here that the Irish Celts could no more be absorbed by American than by British society because they were a "nation separate in blood, separate in religion."[34] In their mixture of racial, religious, and social prejudices against the Irish people, Froude's writings continue to provide rare insights into that mélange of Anglo-Saxonist attitudes which characterized so many members of the English governing classes in the second half of the century.

The most trenchant criticism of Froude's *The English in Ireland* came from the pen of W. E. H. Lecky, who fits less comfortably into the Anglo-Saxonist mold than his adversary in Irish historiography.[35] Unlike Stubbs, Freeman, Green, and Froude, Lecky managed to stay clear of the heady Anglo-Saxonist atmosphere of Oxford except for the award of an honorary degree in 1888. But after 1885, he joined in the campaign against Home Rule with all the resources at his command. Lecky was too perceptive and cosmopolitan an historian to subscribe to a purely racial explanation of human behavior, but he had made up his mind in the 1860's that the Irish people were utterly unfit for self-government, and he never budged from that position in later years. A strong defender of property rights in Ireland and a man who thought the Irish needed firm government "on the Indian model," Lecky once wrote to his old friend, W. J. O'Neill Daunt that

Home Rule would be "the most perfect of all earthly realisations of Pandemonium."[36]

The precocious historian of European rationalism and morals assigned a large role in human affairs to fictions, myths, and ideas; at the same time he did not neglect national character. Referring to the absence of an industrial spirit in Ireland, Lecky observed in his *History of European Morals:*

> The usual characteristic of the latter nation is a certain laxity or instability of character, a proneness to exaggeration, a want of truthfulness in little things, an infidelity to engagements from which an Englishman, educated in the habits of industrial life, readily infers a complete absence of moral principle. But a deeper experience and a larger philosophy soon dispel this error.[37]

Lecky's Irish volumes in his *History of England* were based on several years of painstaking research among the state papers in Dublin and London, and the message he conveyed was that Irish nationhood had flourished in the later eighteenth century because of its intimate connection with an enlightened natural aristocracy made up of Anglo-Irish landowners and graduates of Trinity College, Dublin, whose background and principles he shared. Lecky's Irish patriotism was thus patrician and moderate in the tradition of Henry Grattan. The only Irish nation he recognized as worthy of emulation was that produced by Anglo-Irish, not Celtic, genius, by the likes of Grattan, Flood, Burke, and Charlemont. Having no real sympathy for Catholic, Celtic, and working class Ireland, Lecky identified himself with those leaders of public opinion who had made possible Ireland's finest hour. If the Parnellite agitation really did succeed in driving out the descendants of that Anglo-Irish governing class, then the country would disintegrate into political, social, and economic chaos. Froude's history of Ireland impugned Irish Celtic character; Lecky's history virtually ignored Celtic Ireland, and focused instead on Anglo-Irish Ireland because it contained "the intellect, the property, the respectability of the country."[38]

Lecky's work in Irish history was, of course, far more balanced, judicious, and accurate than Froude's, but he did not, or could not, detach himself from the political realities of his own day while writing about the Ireland of Grattan and Burke; and it was his basic agreement with Froude about the evil workings of democratic nationalism in the country that helped to preserve their friendship from any rift over their conflicting interpretation of Irish history. Lecky not only wrote weighty articles as well as letters to newspapers about the iniquity of Home Rule, but he championed the Unionist cause in Parliament as the member for Dublin University from 1895 to 1902.[39] In his last lengthy book, *Democracy and Liberty* (1896), which was the expression of an embittered conservative rather than a disinterested historian, he fulminated against Irish clericalism and Parnellism in a manner Froude would have approved.[40] "It is curious," Lecky had once written to a close friend, "how Irish affairs turn us all into Tories."[41]

Enough has been said about Anglo-Saxonist historiography to suggest that many of England's leading historians after the mid-century believed that distinctions of race and national character had played a vital role in shaping the past. Green, Stubbs, Smith, Freeman, Kingsley, and Froude all thrived to some extent on the idea of inherent and lasting contrasts between Saxons and Celts, and their ethnocentric prejudices on this score were just as blatant as those of most ethnologists and anthropologists. In the militancy of their Anglo-Saxonism Freeman and James Hunt had much in common. These historians tended to agree that all Celts loved autocratic government as much as Anglo-Saxons cherished those free institutions which derived from an ancient German or Saxon ideal of liberty. Out of this contrast the politically mature and emotionally stable, virile and enlightened Saxon yeoman emerged as an heroic archetype immeasurably superior in all respects to the clannish, primitive, excitable, and feminine Celt. This racial and emotional antithesis contained many reassuring features for those respectable Victorians who were apprehensive about the ability of the Anglo-Saxon race and the capacity of their own class, to survive the growing menace of democratization, social mobility, and alien or Celtic immigration.

CHAPTER VII

Anglo-Saxonism in America

Not the least remarkable feature of these Anglo-Saxonist doctrines is that they appeared almost intact on the other side of the
Atlantic at roughly the same time as they were being articulated in
England. The history of Anglo-Saxonism in the nineteenth century
needs to be written from a comparative Anglo-American point of
view, because the parallels and analogies that emerge from even a
survey of this body of thought in both countries are nothing short of
striking. Almost all the recent evidence provided by American students of nativism points to the fact that Anglo-Saxonism in America
had much in common with its counterpart in England; and this seems
to have been particularly true of the period from the mid-1860's to the
mid-1890's.[1]

If nativism was in some respects a peculiarly American phenomenon that rose and fell in intensity after the mid-nineteenth century,
as John Higham has argued, the specifically ethnocentric dimension
of this movement bore a remarkable resemblance to Anglo-Saxonist
patterns of thought in England. Some of the eminently respectable
exponents of immigration restriction in Boston, New York, and other
eastern metropolitan areas were imbued with the Anglo-Saxonism of
Freeman, Green, Kingsley, and Froude. They shared the same fears
as their English analogues lest the Anglo-Saxon race and culture, of
which they held themselves to be among the finest living representatives, be undermined to the point of ruin by the flood of alien, unassimilable peoples which was sweeping from Europe into America.
Irish immigrants in the late 1840's and 1850's were among the first
wave of impoverished peoples from across the Atlantic to receive the

full brunt of this ethnocentric hostility. The Irish newcomers in Boston during the next three decades touched off in 'Brahmin' minds the same kind of resentment and prejudices which were found among middle and upper middle class Anglo-Saxonists in London, Liverpool, Birmingham, or Manchester. In both cases members of these established classes believed that working class immigrants from Ireland as well as from central and eastern Europe were despoiling if not actually subverting those cities and towns which were considered to be Anglo-Saxon creations. The urban trend of the vast majority of Irish and European immigrants who entered Britain and the United States usually meant that the loudest protests came from educated people who lived in the respectable neighborhoods of those cities and from the indigenous working classes who had to 'suffer' them not just as neighbors but as serious rivals for their jobs.[2]

There were, of course, important differences between Anglo-Saxonist mythology in England and in America, and some of them stemmed from the special development of America from a colonial and frontier society to an advanced industrial and imperial power in the course of little more than a century. Another difference was the incomparably greater volume of immigrant traffic pouring into America in the last third of the nineteenth century. But when all the social, intellectual, political, economic, demographic, and other contrasts between England and America have been weighed and measured, there remains a common core of ethnocentrism which was shared by a number of English and American intellectuals and professional men, who claimed to be Anglo-Saxons and gentlemen by birth and who regarded themselves as members of a cultural elite by virtue of their breeding and their education at such Anglo-Saxonist incubators as Eton and Harrow, Groton and Exeter, Oxford and Cambridge, as well as Amherst, Harvard, Johns Hopkins, Cornell, and Yale.

In mid-nineteenth century America, especially in New England and the mid-Atlantic states, there were many precedents for the kinds of prejudice that Anglo-Saxonists directed against aliens and foreigners. When the newer immigrants happened to be not only destitute but labelled as carriers of socialist or revolutionary doctrines as well as tuberculosis, then the burden of ethnocentrism became all the more intolerable for those who had to shoulder it. A large portion of that burden was, in fact, inspired by Anglo-Saxonism, and it is not difficult to discover signs of this ethnocentric outlook in some of the leading universities during the years just after the Civil War. During the 1870's and 1880's Anglo-Saxonism blossomed into a strident and apologetic creed which was expounded by men of some power and influence in American society. The young Henry Adams, Henry Cabot Lodge, A. Lawrence Lowell, Herbert Baxter Adams, and many others of similar backgrounds took up this mythology with pride and passion.

Some modern historians have called Herbert Baxter Adams, James K. Hosmer, Francis Parkman, and their friends 'Teutonists,' but the label Anglo-Saxonist is more appropriate because the frame of reference and the focus of attention in both English and American historiography had much more to do with the way Anglo-Saxons had developed or perfected ancient German institutions in England and America than with the social, political, and cultural condition of the Goths, Germans, Teutons, or Saxons in the fifth and sixth centuries.[3] Like their English analogues, the American Anglo-Saxonists believed that the free and noble institutions of their two countries were the freest and noblest in the world and that they derived from the inborn and inherited qualities of those peoples who had carried their marks and 'folk-motes' from the Baltic and the Black Forest first to Britain and then, centuries later, across the Atlantic to America. Depending upon their personal predilections and needs, these historians chose to emphasize either the Teutonic or English origins of American liberties. In either case the object was to establish by scientific methods the historical fact of an ethnic and racial as well as cultural continuity from the remote Teutonic past to the immediate American present, and to point out from time to time the present dangers which threatened that Anglo-Saxon heritage.

Some of the American historians who indulged their ethnocentric prejudices in studies of the Saxon or Teutonic origins of the town meeting of colonial America derived their 'facts' from Kemble, Freeman, and Sir Henry Maine. Others owed some of their Anglo-Saxonist theories to graduate study at German universities, above all Göttingen, where they had immersed themselves in the ethnocentric environment which had inspired the writings of Waitz, the Maurers, Mommsen, and Pauli. Others again nourished their Anglo-Saxonism at home in the privacy of their libraries where they could contemplate family trees and ancestral portraits in comfort, far removed from the hordes of Irish Celts and even less desirable immigrants. Some of these American Anglo-Saxonists looked to Darwin's *Origin of Species* and *Descent of Man* and to Galton's work on hereditary genius for scientific confirmation of their beliefs about the evolution of the superior race which they represented. Others found their inspiration in Herbert Spencer and in the racialist theories of those extravagant ethnologists, J. C. Nott and G. R. Gliddon. But they all chose to project their ancestral pride and aristocratic values onto the larger screen of American and even world history; and like their English analogues they too projected their own fantasies and anxieties onto the many new 'strangers in *their* land.'

The Anglo-Saxonist school of history in America prided itself on using the latest scientific methods adopted from German or English models. At Johns Hopkins, Herbert Baxter Adams preached the message of Anglo-Saxon superiority and practiced the writing of present minded history. Blending social Darwinism with Freeman's comparative historical method, Adams inspired and trained a group of specialists in regional and local history whose monographs appeared in his notable series, *The Johns Hopkins University Studies in Historical and Political Science.* Adams would have been the last man, of course, to realize how much more sentiment than science permeated this series. For men like James K. Hosmer, one of H. B. Adams' ardent admirers, the prime function of the scientific historian was to analyze the organism of the body politic, and his own search for "the proper primordial cell of a free Anglo-Saxon state" led him straight to the ancient Teutonic 'folk-mote,' or free, open meeting of the folk or people.[4] Drawing heavily on the work of Waitz and Freeman, Hosmer traced the migration of the 'folk-mote' from England to the New England colonies of the seventeenth century, just as the English Anglo-Saxonists had seen to the transplanting of the mark from German forests to Britain in the sixth century. The student of "primordial cells" in colonial American society had this to say about Celts:

> While multitudes of the ancient stock [in New England] have forsaken the granite hills, their places have been supplied by a Celtic race, energetic and prolific, whose teeming families throng

city and village, threatening to outnumber the Yankee element.
. . . Whatever may be said of the virtues of these newcomers . . .
they have not been trained to Anglo-Saxon self-government. We
have seen the origin of the Folk-mote far back in Teutonic antiquity. As established in New England, it is a revival of a most
ancient thing. The institution is uncongenial to any but Teutonic
men; the Irishman and Frenchman are not at home in it, and
cannot accustom themselves to it, until, as the new generations
come forward, they take on the characteristics of the people
among whom they have come to cast their lot.[5]

The pronounced nostalgia of men like Hosmer for the pure democracy of the New England town meeting, which informed so much of
their historical work, should be interpreted in the context of the pressures of an increasingly urban, industrial, and ethnically mixed society
which appeared to them to threaten their own political, social, economic, and intellectual ascendancy.

Other Anglo-Saxonists of note who spread the historical 'light
and truth' in the 1870's and 1880's were John Fiske, the flamboyant
lecturer who called Freeman "our greatest master in history, almost
the greatest that ever lived"; John W. Burgess, whose race consciousness had been stimulated in Germany and who shared Fiske's nostalgia for the Arcadian democracy of colonial America, although he insisted that the fountainhead of Anglo-Saxon liberties was Germany
not England; Henry Cabot Lodge, whose political career prevented
him from repeating on the platform what he wrote disparagingly
about the Irish Celts as an historian; Albert B. Hart of Harvard; Andrew D. White and Moses C. Tyler of Cornell; and Francis Walker,
president of M.I.T.[6]

The versatile Walker, who managed to be a lawyer, journalist,
economist, and census director as well as a college president, was
more than pessimistic about the ability of Anglo-Saxon culture to
endure or survive the flood of new immigrants pouring into the country. His demographic studies of marriage and fertility patterns among
native and foreign born families convinced him that the non-Anglo-
Saxon elements were steadily outbreeding native Americans. His
reading of the census data led him to believe that these unassimilable
immigrants were spawning children indiscriminately at just that time

when native Anglo-Saxon Americans were beginning to limit their family size by means of contraceptive devices and other methods.[7] Walker's gloomy predictions about the gradual submergence of Anglo-Saxon culture anticipated in some respects those Englishmen who talked and wrote excitedly in the Edwardian period about 'race suicide' or the voluntary limitation of families, especially among the more affluent classes. If the Banks thesis in *Prosperity and Parenthood* about the increasing use of birth control techniques among the middle and upper middle classes in England during the years of the so-called Great Depression has any bearing on the American scene, then one might argue that the Walkers, Fiskes, Adamses, and Hosmers were also concerned with being able to afford the "paraphernalia of gentility" in a time of ever more expensive tastes, schooling, and vacations for the family.[8] For pessimists like Walker the greatest threat to the ascendancy of Anglo-Saxons in America lay in the paraphernalia of poverty, namely droves of ragged children, disease, radical ideas, and contempt for or ignorance of Anglo-Saxon culture. Unless the flow of alien immigrants into America was reduced or limited in some way, men like Walker concluded that their own class or caste would soon be swamped.

Most of these American Anglo-Saxonists were born into comfortable middle and upper middle class homes. They had some private means and were fiercely proud of their pedigrees. In Boston the use of the term Brahmin indicated just how much of a caste these Anglo-Saxonists were considered to be. Some of the men who belonged to this loosely knit 'establishment' of New England and Atlantic-oriented families not only resented the intrusion of proletarian immigrants from eastern and southern Europe but worked hard to restrict that influx. The leading Anglo-Saxonists were patrician intellectuals and publicists, full of romantic notions about the good society that their ancestors had created for the enjoyment of their own flesh and blood, and they found it ever more difficult to share the bounties and rewards of that society with newcomers who could not speak good English let alone understand the Anglo-Saxon heritage that had made the country into a major power. These men were anxious about their status in an age when new money and new men of influence were appearing in all the big cities; they also feared for the integrity of Anglo-Saxon culture. They were the victims of a culture anxiety in so far as they had convinced themselves that the culture in which they had grown up would be ruined by direct contact with the peoples of proletarian Italy, Poland, Russia, Eastern Europe, and Ireland. As John Higham has pointed out, the irony of Anglo-Saxonism in America, and the same can be said of England, was that what had started out as a libertarian creed devised to safeguard the 'ancient liberties' of the free citizen or subject, had become by the second half of the nineteenth century a doctrine of reaction, elitism, and exclusivist ethnocentrism.[9]

The Anglo-Saxonism of American historians and intellectuals in the second half of the nineteenth century differed in few respects, certainly not in kind, from that which Dilke, Freeman, Froude, and other Englishmen were articulating in the 1860's and 1870's. Francis Parkman's declaration that "the Germanic race, and especially the Anglo-Saxon branch of it, is peculiarly masculine, and, therefore, peculiarly fitted for self-government" and his belief that the French Celt was too impulsive and irrational to deserve Anglo-Saxon freedom might have been uttered by Kingsley or Froude.[10] In Maryland in the early 1880's an experiment was launched that sought, in effect, to re-create the mark system of the sixth century which Kemble and Freeman had publicized. Roaming over a large tract of forested land, the boys of McDonogh School were encouraged to stake out hunting grounds and to share in the produce of common land on the basis of what was assumed to be the Teutonic mark system. To such extravagant lengths did some Americans go in order to prove that Anglo-Saxon adolescents had much in common with their primitive Teutonic ancestors.[11]

The more strident tones of some American Anglo-Saxonists may well have been the result of the heavier pressure of immigration and social mobility that weighed on the established classes in America. In both England and America, however, Anglo-Saxonist historians tended to accept the gospel of Social Darwinism, and they shared some of the ethnologists' assumptions about the role of race in determining the position of nations and peoples in the hierarchy of human merit and value.[12] If Darwin's theory of evolution was rapidly distorted in America in order to explain the remarkable development of the country and its people, it did not follow that all Anglo-Saxonists were Social Darwinists. In both England and America Anglo-Saxonism appealed to men who were historians, or who were historically and genealogically minded, and in both cases it became something of a refuge for patricians who resented the pressures of modernization and who found some emotional compensation in not only venerating their own pedigrees but in regarding the Catholic, Celtic Irish, among other alien peoples, as belonging to a race with many undesirable traits.

The post-famine emigration from Ireland aroused fears among many Americans lest Anglo-Saxon culture and society be jeopardized by masses of diseased, penniless, and politicized Irishmen. American Anglo-Saxonists who lived in cities with large Irish populations like Boston, New York, and Philadelphia began by harboring xenophobic and nativist feelings against these Celtic immigrants. By the end of the century, however, they had found other more alien and therefore more threatening groups such as Russian and Polish Jews on which to focus their hostility, and they resorted to racialist arguments with more frequency and acerbity in their campaign to restrict immigration. These new "strangers in the land" faced high barriers of language, custom, race, and creed, behind which not only men of English and northern European stock but also more and more assimilated Irish Americans took refuge.[13]

CHAPTER VIII

The Debate Over Irish Home Rule

Among those Englishmen who were most influenced in their thinking about Ireland and the Irish by the Anglo-Saxonist attitudes of historians and ethnologists were the politically active members of the middle and upper classes who decided to oppose Home Rule in 1886 and thereafter. To these politicians we now turn for some clues about the ways in which the Anglo-Saxonist image of Ireland operated in Westminster. The debates in Parliament and in the metropolitan press over Irish Home Rule reveal some striking examples of the fears that troubled Englishmen whenever the Irish Question came to mind. Almost every Conservative agreed that a Home Rule solution along the lines demanded by Parnell would prove disastrous for both England and Ireland and would shake the empire to its foundations. They were joined in this view by those Whigs, Liberals, and Radicals from Lord Hartington to Joseph Chamberlain who either abstained from or voted against Gladstone's Home Rule Bill in June, 1886.[1] Many anti-Home Rule speeches and pamphlets contained lurid prophecies about the chaos which would inevitably ensue in an independent and, presumably, republican Ireland ruled by Parnell and his band of allegedly criminal followers. Unionist propagandists warned that Irish Catholics would exact their pounds of Protestant flesh in revenge for centuries of persecution by depriving their hereditary enemies of their property and liberty, and possibly even their lives. Some Unionists predicted that Home Rule would plunge Ireland into a civil war that would make Cromwell's massacre of Drogheda look like a minor Irish 'shindy.' Such dire prophecies about the consequences of Home Rule may be seen in their most concentrated form in the tracts and leaflets published in the 1880's and 1890's by the Irish Unionist Alliance and the Irish Loyal and Patriotic Union.[2] These assorted "horrors of Home Rule" were more than artificial devices designed to whip up opposition to a measure that was considered iniquitous. They were the residue of old English prejudices about the Irish, and they both reflected and reinforced Anglo-Saxonist attitudes about the political immaturity and unreliability of Irish Celts.

The debates over Home Rule in 1886 and 1893-94 brought to a head the prolonged controversy about the fitness of the Irish people for self-government. On both occasions the debates in Parliament turned largely on the crucial question as to whether or not Irishmen could be safely entrusted with responsibility for the lives, property, and liberties of their 'Sassenach' enemies in Ireland. The different answers to this question exposed the profound divergence of opinion between the Anglo-Saxonist and the environmentalist views of Irish history and national character. The debates also forced Unionists to air their views about whether the Irish were a relatively pure race, distinctly inferior to the English, or a people who were so mixed in blood that the idea of their constituting a separate and distinct nation was totally false.[3] Although they refrained from relying too heavily on the peculiarities of Irish character as an argument for maintaining the Union, most English Unionists argued that Irish nationalism was the artificial contrivance of a few militant agitators which lacked genuine majority support. They did not mind piling on inconsistencies by arguing that Ireland was not one nation and one people, as Home Rulers often asserted, but two. At the same time these Unionists denied that the southern or Celtic Irish really constituted a separate nation deserving political recognition by the Imperial authority at Westminster. However much Unionists tried for tactical reasons to play down the specifically ethnocentric content of their opposition to Home Rule, their speeches in Parliament tended to reveal the constant interaction of race, class, and religious prejudice, as they tried to grapple with the proposals of Gladstone and his ministers for the final pacification of Ireland.[4]

The most important consequence of the debate over the first Home Rule Bill, apart from its immediate impact on party alignments at Westminster, was to focus attention on the deep chasm between

Anglo-Saxonists, who argued that Irish character made the Irish unfit for self-government, and the environmentalists, who believed in the potential equality of mankind and contended that historical circumstances had made the Irish what they were. Change those conditions, they urged, and the Irish would become as peaceful and law abiding as the English. The Home Rule episode in 1886 forced the environmentalists in the Liberal party to articulate their ideas about Irish history, and for the first time the ethnocentric camp faced a coherent and aroused opposition to their ideas about race.[5]

Unfortunately there is no room here to enter into a detailed discussion of the Home Rule debates in 1886 and 1893-94. The ebb and flow of argument, the powerful set speeches and sharp rebuttals of Gladstone, Morley, Harcourt, Hartington, Goschen, Chamberlain, Hicks Beach and other prominent speakers deserve a chapter to themselves. In general Unionist speakers assumed all along that the Irish were not ready for Home Rule, and the Gladstonian Liberals replied that the Irish had been the unhappy victims of forces beyond their control, and that their natures were no better and no worse than those of any other people in the world.

Gladstone led off the debate in 1886 by declaring that he wished not only to raise the Irish Question high above the din of party politics but to free the discussion from prejudice against the Irish people, who deserved "free institutions" as much as Englishmen or "Scotchmen." Gladstone asserted that the alternation of repressive and conciliatory legislation had been fatal to social order in Ireland; Irish agrarian crime was only the symptom of a political disease which Englishmen had it in their power to cure; and a moderate Home Rule measure would bring peace to Ireland as well as emancipate Parliament from the bane of obstruction. Although he recognized the principle of Irish nationality, he denied the existence of a separate and distinct Irish national character. The Opposition, he declared, condemned Irishmen as unfit to perform civil or political functions in the manner of Europeans and Americans and treated them as either a *lusus naturae* or a people who could understand only "perpetual strife and dissension." Such a view, he said, was founded on a "monstrous misconception."[6] Gladstone perceived the importance to the Unionist cause of the Anglo-Saxonist image of Ireland, and later in the debate he accused G. J. Goschen, the prominent Liberal Unionist, of believing that

Irishmen had "ineradicable and incurable vices" and that they had "a sort of double dose of original sin."[7] Goschen denied this charge, but added that the Irish were not "such an angelic people as to be likely to be suddenly transformed at one stroke of the pen, and all at once endowed with the faculty of governing themselves."[8] John Morley, the new Irish Chief Secretary, challenged his opponents to say openly what many of them were thinking, namely that Ireland was not "ripe for representative institutions."[9] Sir Charles Russell, the Liberal Attorney General, denied that Irish discontent and agrarian crime were the result of the "perversity of the Irish character." That was the kind of argument, he avowed, which J. S. Mill had once called "the weak excuses of imbecile statesmen."[10] Gladstonian Liberals thus appealed for an end to the prejudices which had so long divided England and Ireland. They hoped to reconcile Irish patriotism with a higher allegiance to the unity of the British empire.

In contrast to the Gladstonian message of reconciliation, the Unionist argument against Home Rule in 1886 rested on the assumptions that Irish character could not be changed overnight, that the Irish were bound to abuse any rights or privileges granted to them, and that the British government would find it almost impossible to enforce any of the safeguards in the bill. The gravamen of the Unionist case was that recent as well as past Irish history had shown that the Irish could not be safely entrusted with the management of their own affairs. The incidence of agrarian crime and disorder was cited repeatedly as proof of this point. Ulster Unionists like Colonel Waring and E. Macnaghten sounded the alarm by warning that a nationalist government in Dublin would be bound to persecute Ulster Protestants.[11] Other Unionists like Sir James Fergusson, Walter Long, and Sir Michael Hicks Beach warned that the agents of the Irish National League would make short work of loyalist property in the south of Ireland.[12]

Many Unionist speakers invoked the specter of civil war between Protestant and Catholic, landlord and tenant, and prophecied that dismemberment of the empire would follow upon this dangerous measure. Joseph Chamberlain, in his speech on the first reading of the bill, singled out for attack the exclusion of Irish members from Westminster. He reminded the House that Ireland was divided into two nations, two races, and two religions, and he saw little hope of agreement between them.[13] The Irish, according to most Unionists, could not be trusted to restrain their natural appetites for spoliation and separation from England once they were given Home Rule. Tim Healy's plea for an end to English "assassination literature" which maligned the Irish fell on deaf Unionist ears.[14] The fiery Major Edward Saunderson mocked the Parnellite claim for freedom as the inherent right of the Irish people. "I absolutely deny," he exclaimed, "that any race has the right to be free. I say that history is on my side and that no race is free until it is strong enough and brave enough to be free. England is free because she has fought for her freedom; but if she had not been strong we should now have been slaves."[15] In the best tradition of Carlyle and Froude Major Saunderson believed that Ireland did not deserve to be free until such time as she became strong enough to free herself — an argument that was not lost on members of the Irish Republican Brotherhood and other extremist groups in Ireland.

For all their efforts to wrap their prejudices against Irish Celts in parliamentary language, Unionist spokesmen could not conceal their skepticism about the readiness of the Irish for that self-government which Englishmen enjoyed and deserved. The burden of their message was that the Irish could not be trusted to manage their affairs, let alone anybody else's, and it took months of exhausting debate in 1886 and 1893 and hundreds of columns in *Hansard* to drive that lesson home. Behind the parliamentary rhetoric of the Unionist case lay the sentiments of those ethnologists and historians, novelists and poets, literary reviewers and cartoonists who had contributed something to that Anglo-Saxonist stereotype called Paddy.

An excellent example of the wider context in which the Unionist case should be placed may be found in a speech given by Lord Salisbury, the Opposition leader, at a rally of the National Union of Conservative and Constitutional Associations in St. James's Hall in May, 1886. In the course of his speech Salisbury denied that Ireland was a nation in the sense that it had a united history with common traditions and achievements. He then turned to the question of confidence in the Irish people. Confidence, he declared, depended upon the people in whom one was supposed to confide: "You would not confide free representative institutions to the Hottentots for instance." After disqualifying the Oriental nations and the Russians from this kind of confidence, he was forced to conclude that self-government worked well only with people of the "Teutonic race." The Irish had unfortunately become "habituated to the use of knives and slugs" and therefore could not expect confidence to be placed in them.[16] Salisbury went on to elaborate the reasons for this want of confidence in the Irish; but his audience and posterity remembered only the Hottentot allusion. Although he had not actually called Irishmen Hottentots, as most Home Rulers charged, he had drawn a painfully close analogy, and the friends of Irish nationalism rushed to join in the outcry against this racialist slur. In the resultant hue and cry no one seemed to care about the aspersion cast on the Hottentots, or on the Russians and Chinese. If Salisbury had committed another of his "blazing indiscretions," he had also revealed the core of the Unionist case against Home Rule.

During the second Home Rule Bill crisis of 1893-94 Unionists made more capital out of Irish clericalism than they had in 1886, by citing evidence of clerical intimidation during the split in the Irish parliamentary party and at polling booths; and they also flaunted the slogan "Home Rule means Rome Rule." The old arguments about the defects of Irish character and the absence of a genuine Irish nationality were refurbished and put on display. Once again Gladstone tried to demolish Unionist convictions about the unreliability of the Irish people,[17] and once again Lord Salisbury, speaking this time in the House of Lords, insisted that the "incurable differences" between the Irish and the English rendered the former unfit for the political liberties of more advanced peoples.[18] Gladstone's bill survived the third reading in the Commons through generous use of the closure, only to be defeated by a huge majority in the Lords. What both the debates of 1886 and 1893-94 proved was that a majority of Englishmen, and especially those with education, property, and position in society refused to change their minds about the ingredients of Irish national character. What really killed Home Rule in 1886 and 1894 was the Anglo-Saxonist stereotype of the Irish Celt.

Unfortunately for the cause of Home Rule the environmentalist assault on that stereotype did not reach its peak until after 1893. Although no single refutation of race thinking about the Irish would have saved Gladstone's two measures, it might have given some Unionists pause to think about the similarities rather than differences between Englishmen and Irishmen. Within the space of two years two important works appeared in England on the subject of race and anti-Irish prejudice. William D. Babington published his study, *Fallacies of Race Theories as Applied to National Character* in 1895, and John M. Robertson, the freethinker, friend of Bradlaugh, and a man of rare intellectual virtuosity, saw his book, *The Celt and the Saxon*, into print in 1897. Both authors were environmentalists who explained any differences in human behavior by non-hereditary factors. They stressed the mixture or confusion of races in the world, and they used Theodor Mommsen's travesty of Celtic character in his *History of Rome* to illustrate their arguments about the prevalence of prejudice.[19] For Babington education rather than heredity held the key to character formation, and national character was so changeable that any racial explanation for those changes was baseless. He devoted a chapter to refuting the theory that Englishmen and Irishmen belonged to separate races: the very phrase "the English race" was an anomaly based on wishful thinking and willful ignorance of the mixture of races in Britain.[20] The notion that a distinct Celtic race lived in Ireland was acceptable "alike to the Irish patriot and to the English apologist for English rule." Babington concluded that there were no specifically Celtic virtues or vices and that the only differences between the English and the Irish were the result of environmental factors, not blood or inheritance.

Robertson's remarkably cogent book contained an introductory essay in which he used historical as well as ethnological evidence to dispose of the idea that the Celts of Ireland were a distinct race. "A race," he wrote,

> is such a complex of elements that the traditional assumption of special and rooted mental characteristics becomes simply fantastic when compared with the facts. The theory of race pedigree, in fact, crumbles to nullity in the case of Celts and Teutons just as it does in the case of Hebrews, Moabites, Midianites, Ishmaelites, Heraclidae, and Romans.[21]

Robertson then turned his guns on Anglo-Saxonist prejudices against the Irish which had corrupted one book after another, exposing the distortions of writers like J. R. Green, the Duke of Argyll, Goldwin

Smith, and Froude. Each chapter in this work exploded some myth about the Irish Celt in history and reinforced the environmentalist case for justice for Ireland. Subtitled "A Study in Sociology," Robertson's book might just as well have been called a study in uncommon sense.

Neither the writings of Babington and Robertson nor the occasional exposure of racial fallacies in Edwardian periodicals served to transform English attitudes towards the Irish people.[22] The Anglo-Saxonists among the governing classes showed little willingness after 1900 to unlearn the lessons about Irish Celts taught by the historians, ethnologists, novelists, and publicists whom they had read. The flow of Anglo-Saxonist writings and speeches castigating Irish Celts did, in fact, begin to abate after 1895, but this trend was not the result of a sudden fit of conscience or objectivity on the part of those educated and respectable men who had opposed Home Rule in the past.

The racial element in anti-Irish prejudice fell off somewhat during the 1890's for various reasons, some of which were quite practical. In the first place the disruption of the Irish party over Parnell's liaison with Mrs. O'Shea and the subsequent divorce scandal did much to discredit the Home Rule cause in the eyes of some English and not a few Welsh and Scottish voters. The bitter in-fighting that took place among the remnants of the Irish parliamentary party after 1891 not only tarnished Irish nationalism but helped to lower the pressure of the Irish Question on English parliamentarians once the second Home Rule Bill had been defeated. The marked reduction of Irish agrarian crime during the 1890's also gave Anglo-Saxonists less opportunity to make political capital out of stories of Celtic violence and disorder in Ireland. In addition, the arrival in London of thousands of immigrants from central, eastern, and southern Europe, many of them Jewish, and most of them destitute and demoralized, conjured up a greater menace to the purity of the Anglo-Saxon people than did the Irish Celts.

This menace loomed much larger, of course, in the eyes of American Anglo-Saxonists who looked on with gloom and despair as the waves of emigration out of Russia, Poland, Germany, Austria-Hungary, and Italy broke upon the shores of their beloved New England and New York. That steady flow of 'unassimilable' aliens into America diverted a good deal of ethnocentric hostility away from the Irish-

Americans, who began to look more Anglo-Saxon in comparison with these recent arrivals. The shrill tones of anti-immigration activists in the 1890's and early 1900's in both England and America attest to the animosity and resentment which these immigrants encountered in the ghettoes and slums of London, New York, Boston, and Philadelphia. In London the organization of societies for the prevention of alien immigration was primarily inspired by the influx of Central European Jews, not Irish Celts.[23] The Irish Question also lost ground in English political consciousness because the headlines and leaders of the newspapers were increasingly devoted to the consequences of a "forward" imperial policy and war: such events as the Jameson raid, Fashoda, the war in South Africa, the Russo-Japanese war, and the lethal game of choosing partners within the European alliance system were bound to push the Irish Question into the background where it continued to ferment until the outbreak of the third Home Rule controversy in 1912.

The lessening of the pressure of Irish nationalism on the English political nation did not mean that Anglo-Saxonist prejudices had succumbed completely to environmentalist arguments. The idea of racial determinism lived on in England in forms just as crude and unscientific as those advanced half a century earlier by Gobineau and Knox. The launching of the third Home Rule campaign in 1912 stirred up much of the old Anglo-Saxonist hostility toward the Irish race. As Albert Venn Dicey wrote to his friend, James Bryce, in May of that year, he was constantly meeting "excellent men and women" in London who declared that race was everything. Dicey himself had no doubts about the fact that inherited qualities counted heavily in human behavior, more so in fact than any other qualities acquired by an individual in the course of his lifetime.[24] And yet there was a difference in the content of some Unionist arguments against Home Rule. Arthur Balfour, for example, went out of his way to deny the existence of racial distinction: "The English are not simply Teutonic — still less are the Irish Celtic." If there was no racial frontier between the two peoples, and if there was no question of the superiority or inferiority of either people, Balfour nevertheless argued that Irish nationality was a pure fiction or dream, and he was convinced that Home Rule would lead to "friction, collision of jurisdiction and, in the end, national disintegration."[25] Not all Unionists, of course, shared Balfour's philosophic detachment about theories of racial conflict, but after a generation of use, the arguments of English Unionists, as distinct from Ulster Unionists, against Home Rule did indeed begin to look less crude, if not less prejudiced, than had been the case in 1886.

The embers of racial determinism still glowed in England long after the environmentalists had taken command of the heights of history, ethnology, and other fields of inquiry into the laws governing the universe. H. S. Chamberlain's massive and confused apotheosis of the Teutonic peoples, *The Foundations of the Nineteenth Century*, appeared in English translation in 1910. Having drunk deep of German culture, Chamberlain had become intoxicated with the idea that Goethe was the supreme embodiment of all that was most noble in the noble race of Teutons, and he rambled on for chapters about the proven superiority of the Teutonic races. Not all his English readers considered him a buffoon or an eccentric. James Bryce, who was himself a student of "race sentiment," described Chamberlain as "an able and very learned Anglo-German writer."[26] The best that can be said of Chamberlain's wild notions about race is that he had the charity to include the Celts of Ireland among the Teutonic peoples.

CHAPTER IX

Celticism: The Irish Response

The impact of strident Anglo-Saxonism upon Irish literature and Irish nationalism in the late nineteenth and early twentieth centuries deserves much more thorough treatment than can be provided here; but a brief outline of the counter current which English images of Ireland stimulated in that country and, indeed, in all parts of what might be called, *pace* Dilke, Greater Ireland, may serve to illustrate the contrapuntal nature of Anglo-Irish cultural relations. The dominant Irish response to Anglo-Saxonism, which is called here Celticism, but which might equally well be labeled Gaelicism, had many antecedents before the 1880's and 1890's when it began to blossom into an exotic flower of lasting significance. To quote Yeats, who did much to fertilize that flower with his own brand of Celticism:

"Come near; I would, before my time to go,
"Sing of old Eire and the ancient ways:
"Red Rose, proud Rose, sad Rose of all my days."[1]

In the late Victorian and Edwardian period many Irish men and women sang of old, proud, and sad Celtic Ireland, and they sang as ardently and nostalgically of Cuchulain, Oisin, and Brian Boru as had Thomas Moore when celebrating "The Coming of the Milesians" and Thomas D'Arcy McGee when praising that mighty race in "The Celts." The songs of these modern Irish bards grew ever louder and more replete with myths and folklore, mystical and nationalistic allusions as the century came to a close with the cause of Home Rule still stymied. The repetition in this neo-bardic literature of such themes as war, rebellion, and heroic death made it dramatically clear to some nationalists just which examples of conduct they were supposed to follow. If the popular heroes of Victorian Englishmen were military figures like Wolseley, Roberts, Gordon, and Kitchener, the heroes of Irish men and women in the same period were either legendary figures like Cuchulain, Queen Maev, Finn Mac Cumhal, and Grania, or fighting rebels like Shane O'Neill, Wolfe Tone, and Robert Emmet.

Celticism was an ethnocentric form of nationalism with a strong measure of race consciousness which many Irishmen used to arm themselves against Anglo-Saxonist claims of cultural and racial superiority. Celticism refers to that body of assumptions, beliefs, and myths, which emphasized not only the uniqueness but the sophistication of early Irish culture, and in particular the virtue of ancient Irish political, legal, and social institutions. Celticists also attached much importance to the continuity of Irish blood from the time of the alleged arrival of the Milesians around 1000 B.C. down to the present day.[2] This antithesis or antidote to Anglo-Saxonism provided Irish political leaders with some of the inspiration needed in order to sustain Ireland's claim to be an ancient nation eminently deserving of the independence which the Sassenach had seized centuries ago. There was a good deal of ancestor worship and racial mythology in Celticism, just as much, in fact, as in Anglo-Saxonism. Rare was the meeting of a branch of the Gaelic League, the Gaelic Athletic Association, or the Ancient Order of Hibernians at which there was no allusion to the purity and the antiquity of the Irish race. Whether labeled Celtic, Gaelic, Goidelic, Milesian, or plain Irish, that race possessed qualities and virtues far superior to those of Anglo-Saxons. According to the Celticist authorities, the high and holy culture of ancient Ireland had been crushed by ruthless, barbarous invaders from Britain and northern Europe, and the most barbarous of them all had been the rapacious Anglo-Saxons and Anglo-Normans, better known in Ireland as "bloody brutal Sassenachs."[3]

In its ethnology and historiography Celticism was essentially separatist and exclusive, refusing to admit that anything good had come from England, except perhaps coal. Lacking so many of the tangible outlets of Anglo-Saxonists in the form of worldwide economic and imperial assets as well as great power status and lacking, too, the quintessential fact of sovereign national independence, the champions of Celticism kept up a much steadier flow of ethnocentric sentiments through the media of books, articles, newspapers, journals, plays, and lectures as well as clubs and associations. Dozens of organizations were launched in the nineteenth century throughout Greater Ireland which were dedicated to the preservation and promotion of Gaelic, Celtic, or Irish culture.[4] The most important difference between English and Irish forms of ethnocentrism was that Anglo-Saxonism represented the mythology of a people who were largely self-fulfilled in a nationalist as well as material and imperial sense. England was a nation, no matter how deep the divisions of class, party, and sect might be. Celticism, on the one hand, was the ethnocentric expression of a people still in the throes of a profound nationalist struggle who were determined to achieve the kind of independence from Westminster which Anglo-Saxonism explicitly denied them. Celticism thus flowed into the main political channel of Irish nationalism, and it sustained the agitation for the return of Ireland's ancient Celtic liberties. Anglo-Saxonism, on the other hand, served the useful function of transferring the more personal and immediate anxieties of Englishmen about their own well-being onto the more abstract and impersonal plane of assumed threats to their ancient liberties and Anglo-Saxon culture. The absence from the Irish scene of a stereotype of English character as rigid and elaborate as Paddy shows that projection played a smaller role in Celticist thinking. For most Celticists the real enemy was as much that impersonal force "English rule" as it was John Bull.

The varieties and extent of Celticism in Ireland, England, and America, not to mention Pan-Celticism in Western Europe, have yet to be explored in depth, and here it is possible only to sketch the outlines of a movement that was as rich in talent as it was in mythology. Like all revivals, whether classical, Gothic, romantic, or otherwise, the Celtic revival of the late nineteenth century had no sharply defined beginning, middle, or end. George Moore, in his caustic reminiscences, *Hail and Farewell*, quoted his friend Edward Martyn as saying: "Ninety-nine is the beginning of the Celtic Renaissance." To this Moore replied: "I am glad to hear it; the Celt wants a renaissance and badly; he has been going down in the world for the last two thousand years."[5] Now Martyn might be excused for trying to connect the Irish renaissance with the acceptance of his own play for production by Yeats' new Irish Literary Theater; but what he ignored was the number of Celtic revivals which had occurred in the three centuries before the performance of *The Heather Field* and Yeats' *The Countess Cathleen* in the Antient Concert Rooms, Dublin, in 1899. The sources of the last great revival, which was made memorable by Yeats, Lady Gregory, AE, Synge, Hyde, Martyn, O'Grady, Sigerson — to mention only the most obvious — reach far back into Irish history, back to those bards, poets, and holy story tellers who were responsible for such classics as the *Táin Bo Cuailgne* and the *Annals of the Four Masters*.[6] Geoffrey Keating's eloquent *History of Ireland,* which was written in Irish in the early seventeenth century, also provided the Celticists of the 1890's and after with much the same kind of evidence about the remote Irish past which Anglo-Saxonists had extracted from Tacitus, Bede, and Giraldus Cambrensis in order to support their own foregone conclusions.[7]

The most important source of Celticism in the eighteenth century was the Celtic or 'Celtic-English' revival which began in the 1750's and 1760's with the poems of Thomas Gray, William Mason, James Macpherson, and Evan Evans who specialized in creating a mood of noble melancholy out of Celtic druids, bards, and warriors. That revival was almost entirely couched in the English language, and judged by the standards of *Ossian,* it was distinguished by a specious style and content. The revival had relatively little to do with Ireland and Irish myths, being heavily Scottish and Welsh in its orientation, not least because of the powerful stimulus provided by Macpherson, Scott, and Burns.[8]

By contrast, the Celtic revival of the late nineteenth century was far more Irish in content, authorship, and language — although English continued to be the dominant medium — and it was much more nationalist in tone than its predecessor. It was also more indebted to the work of Celtic folklorists, philologists, and archaeologists as well as to political writers like the men of Young Ireland. This climactic Celtic revival owed a great deal of its thrust to the organization of Irishmen and women — poets, publicists, journalists, popular historians, and dreamers — into countless societies and associations which flourished in the second half of the century. The founding of the Ossianic Society in Dublin in 1853, the Irish Literary Society of London in 1891, the National Literary Society of Dublin in 1892, the

Royal Society of Antiquaries of Ireland in 1890,[9] and the Gaelic
League in 1893, to mention but a few examples, reflected in part the
trend toward increasing political organization in both England and
Ireland in this period. But the immediate inspiration of these new
societies was literary and scholarly, and among their patrons could be
found aristocrats like the Marquis of Ormonde and the 2nd Earl of
Dunraven as well as scrupulous Irish scholars of a more middle class
hue like Eugene O'Curry, John O'Donovan, and George Petrie. In
France the *Revue Celtique* founded in 1870, and later edited by the
noted Celticist D'Arbois de Jubainville, and in Germany the *Zeit-
schrift für Celtische Philologie* founded in 1896 by Kuno Meyer and
L. C. Stern provided a foundation of impressive and cosmopolitan
scholarship on which less erudite Celticists could build their raths,
dolmens, and castles.[10] All of these societies and journals helped to
put together that synthesis of philology, history, mythology, folklore,
and fantasy which is called here Celticism.

The Celticist response to Anglo-Saxonism in the late Victorian
period drew some of its historical inspiration from the topographical
sections of the famous Irish Ordnance Survey, launched by Sir
Thomas Larcom in the 1830's and aborted by the British government
in the early 1840's. It derived some of its vigor and lyrical quality
from the poetry and prose of Thomas Davis, Thomas D'Arcy McGee,
and Clarence Mangan which contained among other derivatives a
hard core of Gaelic or Celtic legend. Along with Charles Gavan
Duffy these fervent young nationalists wished to provoke the readers
of their weekly journal *The Nation* into equal fervor by making it
"racy of the soil."[11]

Young Ireland was not as exclusive in its ethnocentrism as were
the more militant nationalists of the early twentieth century because,
as Davis declared in his poem "Celts and Saxons," it was time for Irish
Celts and Irish Saxons to unite and make common cause against English Saxons.[12] Celticism also owed something to the Fenians of the
1860's, whose choice of name revealed an awareness of Irish mythology and whose nationalist views were animated by a strong note of
ethnocentrism. Above all, Celticism depended for much of its content and inspiration on the growing body of folklore, myth, legend,
and superstition which was being collected and published in Dublin
and London in the last decades of the century.[13] Such were some of

the roots of that 'wild rose' which blossomed in the 1890's with the coming together of those gifted, indeed inspired, men and women who made the Irish literary renaissance what it was. Theirs was the supreme expression of Celticism. Apart from the early poems and plays of Yeats as well as his *Celtic Twilight* (1893), one may cite such examples of this "racy" ethnocentrism as Lady Gregory's *Gods and Fighting Men* (1904) and the collection of Celticist essays she edited, *Ideals in Ireland* (1901), George Sigerson's *Bards of the Gael and Gall* (1897), Sophie Bryant's *The Genius of the Gael* (1913), Douglas Hyde's *A Literary History of Ireland* (1898), Alice Stopford Green's *The Making of Ireland and its Undoing* (1908), and Edmund Hogan's *The Irish People* (1899). Heavy deposits of Celticism may also be found in *The Leader*, edited by that apostle of Irish Ireland, D. P. Moran, in the files of the *Irish Peasant* once it had fallen into the editorial hands of W. P. Ryan, in the pages of *The New Ireland Review*, and also in the 'Ossianized' poetry of Fiona Macleod, otherwise known as William Sharp. The official organs of the Gaelic League and the Irish Literary Theater shared with *The Gaelic Journal* and Arthur Griffith's *United Irishman* a distinctly Celticist flavor.[14]

One of the most forceful statements of the Celticist position was Hyde's lecture "The Necessity for De-Anglicising Ireland," delivered in Dublin in 1892. In the course of his address Hyde implored the sons of the noble Gaelic race to throw off the insidious culture of the Saxon and to return to a pure Irish culture by learning "our once great national tongue."[15] Hyde was preaching the same kind of cultural purity that Freeman had done in his Anglo-Saxonist way twenty or thirty years earlier. Both men were equally sensitive to the corrupting influences they saw at work in their respective cultures, and both were equally absolutist in the remedies they prescribed. The Irish and Anglo-Irishmen who made possible this cultural revival were convinced that in order to create a new Ireland and to animate it with a new Celtic spirit they had to rediscover the old Ireland of pre-conquest times through both folklore and history. To some extent they found an escape from such paraphernalia of modernity as Dublin Castle bureaucrats, land judges, Congested Districts Board officials, school inspectors, and scientific agriculturists in ancient bards and heroic warriors. In their enthusiasm for uncovering 'hidden' Gaelic Ireland, they underestimated the difficulties of the Irish language, and, uninhibited by the learning of Zeuss or Meyer, they plunged ahead into the thickets of that language often insensible to the errors in grammar, spelling, meaning, and pronunciation which they left in their wake.[16]

In spite of their denials of political intent Hyde and his associates in the Gaelic League were far more 'political' than they cared to admit. That is to say, they were politicized intellectuals rather than partisan nationalists. The Celticism of their writings and speeches furnished their more politically active contemporaries with many of the materials of a separatist movement. Nothing was easier than for a militant nationalist — and there were many degrees of militancy in Ireland after the fall of Parnell — to interpret Hyde's arguments about "de-Anglicising" Ireland in a purely political context.[17]

Like the Anglo-Saxonists, the Celticists also had their fictional historians or historical myth-makers who spun out of a few thin threads an elaborate tapestry depicting a social and political Arcadia in Ireland before the coming of the Sassenach. Alice Green carried forward her late husband's Home Rule sympathies, but she betrayed the Anglo-Saxonist legacy of *The Short History* repeatedly in her writings on Irish history. Ancient Ireland, she once asserted, was a "true democracy — a society in which ever broadening masses of the people are made intelligent sharers in the national life, and conscious guardians of its tradition."[18] The theory of the Milesian origins of the Irish accomplished for Celticist historians what the Teutonic origins theory had done for Anglo-Saxonists. Irish historians found in the sept and communal property rights in ancient Ireland their equivalent of the mark system; and in gavelkind they saw a practice superior to English laws of primogeniture.[19] If Celticist ethnology was much less scientific than its Anglo-Saxonist counterpart, it contained the same emphasis on tracing the distinct as well as distinctly superior qualities of the Irish or Celtic race. Despite the painful invasions, plantations, and migrations in Irish history, despite all of Ireland's vaunted contacts with the Continent before the twelfth century, the so-called native Irish were still held to be pure of blood. Genealogists like John O'Hart traced the pedigree of Irish kings and chieftains straight back in an unbroken line to Adam.[20] Both Celticist poetry and history carried the message that a rich mixture of Milesian, Firbolgian, Tuatha de Danann and Gaelic blood flowed in Irish veins, unblemished by Saxon, Norman, Danish or any other non-Celtic blood.

Needless to say the Celticists, too, had their lunatic fringe made up of patriots who insisted on racial purity or who declared that America had been discovered in the year 545 by that great Christian missionary, St. Brendan, Bishop of Clonfert.[21] But these myths were innocuous by comparison with those of Gobineau, Knox, and H. S. Chamberlain. By means of associations and meetings as different in tone and patronage as the Pan-Celtic Society (1888), the Irish Race Convention (1897), and the Pan Celtic Congress (1901) the Celticists assembled a self-image of the Irish people that was as flattering to the believer as the one put together by Anglo-Saxonists a generation or so earlier.[22] The so-called genius of the Gael or Celt was as emotionally satisfying to many Irishmen as the genius of the Anglo-Saxon had been and continued to be for many of their English contemporaries.

If the Celticists in Ireland lacked historians of the eminence of Freeman, Stubbs, Green, and Froude, they could boast of many more journals and societies specifically dedicated to the promotion of all things Celtic, Gaelic, or Irish. Hyde's agitation of the language question was fully exploited by Arthur Griffith, Padraic Pearse, and many other nationalists of the post-Parnellite generation; and Eoin Mac-Neill carried the cause forward from his position in the new National University of Ireland. Sinn Fein was in some respects the political expression of this Celticist revival: its name, its emphasis on self-reliance and pride in race, and its increasing resort to proclamations, titles of address, and names in Irish showed that its leaders were not insensitive to the work of Hyde and his Gaelic Leaguers. The Celticist message of pride in race and culture was not only heard but repeated endlessly in Irish-American communities across the Atlantic; and societies for preserving and promoting the Irish language sprang up in the major cities of the eastern seaboard, notably in New York and Boston.[23] After the fall of Parnell, and throughout the period of constant feuding within the Irish parliamentary party, more and more young Irishmen succumbed to the Celticist attractions of the G.A.A., the A.O.H., the I.R.B., and, eventually, Sinn Fein wherein Irish history and mythology were inseparable. Irish nationalism had, indeed, become "racy of the soil," or, rather, 'racy of the race.'[24]

Celticism thus helped many Irishmen to defend themselves against Anglo-Saxonist slurs and to arm themselves with a form of cultural self-respect on the strength of which they sought to oppose or defy the imperial authority at Westminster. Patterns of ethnocentric thinking, and especially pride in the Irish race, could be found in all the more extreme organizations from the Gaelic Athletic Association and the Irish Republican Brotherhood, to the Dungannon Clubs, Cumann na nGaedheal, and, after 1907, the Sinn Fein movement led by Griffith. Modern Irish nationalism was, of course, a mosaic made up of many beliefs and goals, a number of which conflicted with one another, but the Celticism of the late nineteenth century helps to explain not only the decline in prestige and effectiveness of the Irish parliamentary party, but the increasingly separatist trend of nationalist thought, especially after the new Liberal government of 1906 had made it clear that Home Rule was not the first item on its agenda. The repudiation by Sinn Fein and other immoderate groups of the constitutional agitation carried on by Redmond and his party was as much a condemnation of the policy of playing the English game of parliamentary process under English rules as it was a rebuke to Redmond and his lieutenants for becoming too 'Anglicised' at Westminster. It is significant that Padraic Pearse found the finest embodiment of the Irish race in Wolfe Tone, not O'Connell or Parnell, and he did so because Tone had been willing to sacrifice his life for the principles in which he believed.[25] Celticism was an expression of both nationalist frustration and cultural striving. It stimulated as well as nourished the appetite of many Irishmen for a sense of cultural and racial solidarity; and by so doing it enabled a few of them, a mere handful in fact, to fight more boldly not only for their country but their race. The belief of many 'physical force' men in the purity and nobility of their Celtic blood made the 'blood sacrifice' of Easter, 1916, all the more an act of racial pride and all the less a gesture of political despair.

CHAPTER X

Conclusion

The ethnocentric antitheses of Anglo-Saxonism and Celticism not only lasted well into the twentieth century, but also helped to aggravate the already strained political relations between England and Ireland to the point of rebellion, guerrilla war, and a treaty that left no party wholly satisfied. In England the embers of Anglo-Saxonism were fanned into flames from time to time. Just before the outbreak of the Boer War there was a good deal of talk about a triple alliance between England and the Teutons of Germany and the Anglo-Saxons of America. The same body of prejudices served in a more negative way to buttress the Unionist case against Home Rule in 1912 and thereafter. The distinction drawn by Lord Salisbury in 1898 between the "living" and the "dying" nations, the pan-Teutonic coat which Joseph Chamberlain trailed before a suspicious German government in the same year, and his high hopes of an "Anglo-Saxon alliance" with America suggest that the idea of a *Pax Teutonica* or *Anglo-Saxonica* had a powerful appeal to some of the more eminent later Victorians.[1] But Anglo-Saxonism was not strong enough to overcome the obstacles in the way of a "Union of the Teutonic Peoples," and it did not prevent the formation of that hybrid alliance after 1902 of English Anglo-Saxons, Japanese Mongols, Russian Slavs, and French Gauls against the predominantly Teutonic central powers, the result of which was the holocaust of 1914-18. The theory that nations like institutions and, indeed, all living things went through distinct stages of organic growth and decay continued to be a necessary belief for those Englishmen who feared, but usually refused to admit publicly, that the signs of decay in their own country indicated senility.

In Ireland the current of Celticism ran faster and carried more and more nationalists ever further away from the world of too harsh realities and too difficult detachment. Appealing irresistibly to politicized poets and to poetic politicians, Celticism helped to build a separatist movement out of different generations and disparate interests. It formed a bridge between the I.R.B. and the Irish language revival which many young men were to cross. The revolution planned and launched by Pearse and his associates in 1916 culminated with the expulsion of the Gall or Sassenach and most of his baggage in 1921. But if Celticist nationalism had won the day, it was not strong enough to keep the peace, and from 1922 to 1924 the hand of Gael was turned against Gael; and the scars of that fratricide are visible in the Irish body politic to this day.

While Celticism provided much of the inspiration and propaganda, the immediate stimuli of the Easter Rising had to do with such specific conditions as the agitation over the Home Rule Bill of 1912, the organization of Ulster into a para-military province trained to fight for 'Protestant Unionism' and against 'Catholic separatism', the readiness of Unionists in high civil and military positions to flirt with rebellion, and growing resistance to the recruitment campaign in Ireland after 1914. The rival ethnocentrisms of Englishmen and Irishmen in an era of world war made it all the easier for political events like these to polarize individuals as well as parties in both countries to a point of no compromise. Celticism provided no panacea for the many material problems which the leaders of the Free State had to face, but it did serve to bind up some of the wounds of the civil war, and it supplied an ideal framework into which one could conveniently fit all of ancient and modern Irish history.

The idea of the racial purity or homogeneity of the Irish people lives on in Ireland not just because few Irishmen have accepted the reality of ethnic diversity or hybridity as demonstrated by the text and morphological tables of *The Physical Anthropology of Ireland*, based on a field study carried out by several eminent Harvard anthropologists in the 1930's,[2] but because the emotional investment in that myth continues to serve some of the same functions today that it did in pre-independence Ireland.

In England Anglo-Saxonism survived the Great War, and could be found in less concentrated forms among those who yearned for the glory and grandeur of the late Victorian empire. It helped to compensate some Englishmen for the loss of their sons and male relatives and also for the loss of their imperial self-confidence. Lord Milner went so far as to publish his version of Anglo-Saxonism, which he called the creed of "British race patriotism," in the columns of the *Times*,[3] but other Englishmen were more reticent about proclaiming this faith. With the Irish Question almost, but never quite, out of the way, Anglo-Saxonists found other suitable targets in India, Asia, and Africa on which they could project their own fears and anxieties.

The idea of race as the biological force that had shaped human history and determined the hierarchy of countries and civilizations in the world gained many adherents in the British Isles in the second half of the nineteenth century. Eminent and obscure Victorians, all of them intolerant to some degree, who were looking for a simple, unalterable, and universal affirmation of the superiority of English or Anglo-Saxon civilization, clung to the notion of hierarchy and worth among the races of man, and they refused to look for the similarities, both physical and mental, between themselves and Irishmen, not to mention peoples with even darker skins than the 'Black Irish.' As part of their search for a reassuring self-image, one that would help to relieve them of some of the strain of living in a highly competitive society with worldwide responsibilities, these Anglo-Saxonists felt compelled to magnify the assumed differences between themselves and the Irish Celts, and the result of that magnification was a caricature of Irish character that answered some of their more pressing emotional needs. These two images of the self and the Celt were as mutually necessary in Anglo-Saxonist minds as the two sides of a coin: the one could not be relinquished without the other.

By forging a great chain of racial being that linked them biologically as well as historically with their highly idealized Saxon or German ancestors, to whom they attributed in embryonic form their own virtues and free institutions, these ethnocentrists found substantial relief from the strain of having to govern people at home and abroad who did not accept the assurances of Her Majesty's Government that British imperial rule stood for liberty and justice for all regardless of race, color, creed, and social class. In the long run belief in the law of the hereditary transmission of character and convictions about the inborn superiority of the Anglo-Saxon proved to be a flimsy protection against the more forceful arguments and weapons of aroused nationalists in various parts of the empire.

Only an emotionally charged pattern of thinking that postulated the 'dearness' of the Anglo-Saxon race and the 'cheapness' of the Celts can explain the tenacity with which so many English Unionists fought to preserve Anglo-Saxon ascendancy in Ireland — an ascendancy that was epitomized in their minds by the Act of Union. That nucleus of ethnocentric attitudes and beliefs which made up Anglo-Saxonism had accounted for so much of the 'magic' with which Englishmen had managed to rule millions of people the world over that it blinded many of the political elite to the realities of colonial nationalism and to the capacities of those nationalist leaders, whether in Ireland or India, to manage the affairs of their countries in their own non-Anglo-Saxon way.[4] The very ethnocentrism of those men who administered the new British empire in the nineteenth century had the effect of awakening or reactivating counter-ethnocentric impulses among their colonial subjects, not least because these 'natives' had to endure constant reminders of their own inferiority in the eyes of the Anglo-Saxons whose orders and edicts they were supposed to obey.

The irony, at times futility, of Anglo-Saxonist attitudes towards Ireland is that they drove a number of Irish men and women to fabricate their own mythology of racial and cultural superiority; and they proved so adept at this myth-making that the English government was eventually forced to concede amidst bloodshed and bitter feelings what they might just as well have conceded in more auspicious, if awkward, circumstances years before. G. M. Young was wide of the mark when he asserted that the reason for the failure of the English in Ireland was their inability to recognize that "time and circumstance had created an Irish mind."[5] As Anglo-Saxonists saw it, not just time but blood and race had created an Irish Celtic mind, which some called Paddy, and the trouble was that none of the conciliatory legislation in the power of Westminster, least of all Home Rule, would ever change that mind for the better.

There are, of course, many facets of Anglo-Saxonism, and its ethnocentric counterpart in Ireland, which remain to be explored, and some of the more inaccessible ones have to do with the contrasts between English stereotypes of Irish behavior and the reality from which they were extracted. More thought should be given to the ways in which Irishmen tried to act out in the presence of Englishmen their own notions of how the Sassenach expected the Celt or Gael to behave.[6] More attention should be paid to the similarities between Anglo-Saxonist images of Irishmen, African or American Negroes, and their own working classes, not to mention such equally 'subordinate' categories as women and children.[7]

There is also an important imperial dimension of Anglo-Saxonist prejudice that deserves further reflection. If many educated Victorians actually believed in the existence of a wide racial and cultural gap between themselves and Irish Celts, then how much more profound a gulf must have separated them from the Indian, African, and Asian peoples over whom they held formal or informal sway. The ethnocentric ladder on which the races of the world had their assigned positions in Anglo-Saxonist eyes must have been much longer than is usually assumed, if the Irish occupied a position little more than half-way between the Anglo-Saxons at the top and the Hottentots at the bottom. Since Anglo-Saxonists accused Irishmen of being unstable, childish, violent, lazy, feckless, feminine, and primitive, and since they likened them to Hottentots, Maoris, Chinese, pigs, apes, and chimpanzees, one may well wonder what epithets, adjectives, and similes were left in the Anglo-Saxonist vocabulary to characterize men of darker skin and more primitive cultures.

No one enjoys the experience of living through the deflation of long cherished myths, especially when those myths touch the very nerve center of the 'national being' and suffuse the whole body of national history and popular lore. To expect Irish Celticists to have been any readier than English Anglo-Saxonists were to abandon their ethnocentric defenses in favor of an environmentalist and relativist view of the peoples and cultures of the world would be utterly unrealistic, not to say unfair. It was far easier, in fact, for Englishmen after 1914 and Irishmen after 1916 to sacrifice their blood in the name of their race and country than it was for either people to sacrifice the idea of the sanctity, purity, and superiority of that blood and the race through which it ran.

Notes

Chapter I

1. R. Koebner, *Empire* (Cambridge, 1961); R. Koebner and H. D. Schmidt, *Imperialism . . . 1840-1960* (Cambridge, 1964).

2. Definitions of ethnic prejudice usually invite more questions than they resolve, but Gordon Allport's interpretation provides a serviceable definition of some of the phenomena considered here: "Ethnic prejudice is an antipathy based upon a faulty and inflexible generalization. It may be felt or expressed. It may be directed toward a group as a whole, or toward an individual because he is a member of that group." *The Nature of Prejudice* (New York, 1958), p. 10. See also Bruno Bettelheim and Morris Janowitz, *Dynamics of Prejudice* (New York, 1950).

3. N. Gash, *Politics in the Age of Peel* (London, 1960), p. ix.

4. G. M. Young, *Victorian England, Portrait of an Age* (London, 1964), p. 186. Here I take issue with Dr. N. Mansergh's assertion in *The Irish Question, 1840-1921* (London, 1965), pp. 48-55, that the "inertia and indifference of English opinion and government" towards Ireland was due chiefly to ignorance. Although he has the support of Nassau Senior in this belief, I would argue that this ignorance was willful or wishful, the result not of insufficient information about Ireland or of inadequate opportunities of learning about the Irish people, but of a deliberate refusal to investigate the Irish question from any but an ethnocentric point of view. Any Englishman anxious to repair his deficiencies in this respect could have found endless data and testimony about Ireland in the many parliamentary commissions and committees of inquiry, as Dr. Mansergh himself admits. Those Englishmen who were seriously interested in learning about the habits of the Irish people need have travelled only so far as the nearest Irish ghetto in city or town, or they might have talked sympathetically with their own Irish domestic servants. The inescapable fact is that most English policy makers *chose* to ignore the realities as distinct from the appearances of Irish life and character. If this was ignorance, it was ignorance born of ethnic prejudice, about which Dr. Mansergh's book is curiously silent. In most other respects this book deserves close attention from students of Anglo-Irish relations.

5. The term 'ethnocentrism' was first used by William Graham Sumner in *Folkways* (Boston, 1906), where he defined it as "this view of things in which one's own group is the center of everything, and all others are scaled and rated with reference to it. . . . Each group nourishes its own pride and vanity, boasts itself superior, exalts its own divinities, and looks with contempt on outsiders." *Ibid.*, p. 13.

6. See T. W. Adorno et al., *The Authoritarian Personality*, Parts One and Two (New York, 1950, 1964), and R. Christie and P. Cook, "A Guide to Published Literature Relating to the Authoritarian Personality Through 1956," *Jo. of Psychology*, 45 (1958), pp. 171-99.

7. For some of this definition I am indebted to Daniel J. Levinson's chapter, "The Study of Ethnocentric Ideology," in *The Authoritarian Personality*, ed. T. W. Adorno et al., Part I, pp. 102-104, 145-50.

8. See for example John Higham, *Strangers in the Land: Patterns of American Nativism* (New Brunswick, 1955), Barbara M. Solomon, *Ancestors and Immigrants* (Cambridge, Mass., 1956), and Edward N. Saveth, *American Historians and European Immigrants, 1875-1925* (New York, 1948). All three works contain many examples of the ethnocentric responses I have in mind.

9. John R. Green, *A Short History of the English People* (London, 1895), pp. 1-2.

10. *Ibid.*, p. 2.

11. The importance of Tacitus' description of the Germani as a source for Anglo-Saxonist historiography can hardly be exaggerated. Every serious student of the ancient ancestors of the Anglo-Saxons, from Montesquieu in the *Esprit des Lois* to Herbert Baxter Adams in his study, *The Germanic Origins of New England Towns* (1883) drew on Tacitus. See the popular edition of *The Agricola and Germany of Tacitus*, eds., A. J. Church and W. J. Brodribb (London, 1899).

12. *Hansard*, 3S, 14, pp. 1044. Bulwer described Germany as "the fatherland of liberty" to which Europe owed its peace and England owed its "dear-bought glory."

13. This definition of Anglo-Saxonism is, of course, a composite one. Not all Anglo-Saxonists subscribed rigidly to these five articles. Some were doctrinaire, some believed in a blander version of the creed, and a few were occasional conformists.

14. See C. Hill's pioneering essay, "The Norman Yoke" in *Puritanism and Revolution* (London, 1962), pp. 50-122.

Chapter II

1. Compare the translations of this passage which may be found in Thomas Wright's edition of *The Historical Works of Giraldus Cambrensis*, translated by Thomas Forester (London, 1892), with that in F. P. Barnard, *English History from Contemporary Writers: Strongbow's Conquest of Ireland* (London, 1910). According to Forester: "This people, then, is truly barbarous, being not only barbarous in their dress, but suffering their hair and beards to grow enormously in an uncouth manner, just like the modern fashion recently introduced; indeed, all their habits are barbarisms." p. 125. According to Barnard: "Wherefore this is a race of savages: I say again a race of utter savages. For not merely are they uncouth of garb, but they also let their hair and beards grow to outrageous length, something like the newfangled fashion which has lately come in with us. In short, all their ways are brutish and unseemly." p. 149. Barnard's interpretation of the word *gens* and its appurtenances in this passage was presumably designed for English schoolboys like those at Reading School of which he was Headmaster. Needless to say, Giraldus hardly ventured outside the Anglo-Norman Pale when he was in Ireland.

2. For discussion of these writers see E. M. Hinton, *Ireland Through Tudor Eyes* (Philadelphia, 1935) and D. B. Quinn, *The Elizabethans and the Irish* (Ithaca, 1967).

3. Edward D. Snyder once collected a number of derogatory adjectives which were directed against the 'ethnic minorities' in the British Isles during the 17th and 18th centuries. See his article "The Wild Irish: A Study of some English Satires against the Irish, Scots, and Welsh," *Modern Philology,* 17 (April, 1920), pp. 147-85.

4. G. M. Young perceived the difficulty of trying to anatomize anti-Irish prejudice when he wrote: "To analyse the Irish trouble into racial, religious, and agrarian is impossible, because in Irish history these three are one, and when England had conceded Catholic Emancipation against her own Protestants, and agrarian reforms against the Irish landlords and both in vain, the logic of history left her no alternative but to concede all the rest, never quite understanding what it was the Irish wanted nor why they wanted it." *Early Victorian England* (London, 1934), II, p. 451.

5. Philip D. Curtin interprets the word 'race' in this sense — without assigning any date for this usage — in his book, *The Image of Africa* (London, 1965), p. 28. For his discussion of earlier race theories in England about the origin of man, and the African in particular, see pp. 28-57, 227-43, 363-87.

6. A. Montagu, *Man's Most Dangerous Myth: The Fallacy of Race*, 4th edn., Meridian Books (1965). See especially pp. 23-82, 117-223. There is

a cogent discussion of race-thinking in the nineteenth century in H. Arendt, *The Origins of Totalitarianism* (London, 1962), pp. 158-221.

7. Among the more important contributions to this long and voluminous debate on the origins of the inhabitants of the British Isles were: Luke Owen Pike, *The English and Their Origin* (London, 1866), Edwin Guest, *Origines Celticae* (London, 1883), Nottidge C. Macnamara, *Origin and Character of the British People* (London, 1900), W. C. Mackenzie, *The Races of Ireland and Scotland* (Paisley, 1916), and the revealing articles on the Celts and Irish ethnology in various editions of *The Encyclopaedia Britannica*, especially the eleventh edition (Cambridge, 1910), V, pp. 611-22. An article on this subject is being prepared for publication.

8. An example of this distinction between racial and national integrity or coherence is provided by Sir Robert Anderson, an Anglo-Irish product of Trinity College, Dublin, who was Assistant Commissioner of Police at the time of the Special Commission in 1888. In his partisan memoir, *Sidelights on the Home Rule Movement* (London, 1906), Anderson flatly denied the existence of an Irish nation because "the population of Ireland is not homogeneous." The racial differences in Ireland were not disappearing, as they tended to do in other countries, but they were instead being "maintained and accelerated by religious strife." See pp. 188-89.

9. See for example A. A. Roback, *A Dictionary of International Slurs* (Cambridge, Mass., 1944), Eric Partridge, *A Dictionary of Slang and Unconventional English* (New York, 1938), and F. H. Grose, *A Classical Dictionary of the Vulgar Tongue* (London, 1785).

10. A few of these attitudes may be found in Philip Mason, *Prospero's Magic* (London, 1962). See especially Chapter 1 on "Class Consciousness and Imperial Aloofness" and Chapters 4 and 5.

11. See A. Montagu, *op. cit.*, pp. 117-32.

12. For an analysis of the social composition of the Parnellites, see C. C. O'Brien, *Parnell and His Party* (Oxford, 1957), pp. 11-23, 150-58. As Dr. O'Brien has shown, only 50 percent of the Irish parliamentary party belonged to his category of "upper group" after the general election of 1885, as compared with 79 percent in 1880. Most of the new Parnellite members in 1885 belonged to O'Brien's "lower group" made up of the lower professions, farmers, shopkeepers, wage-earners, etc. Anxiety about social status among the self-conscious middle classes may well have been aggravated by the presence of these socially inferior Irishmen in the House of Commons.

13. Quite apart from working class prejudice in Britain against Irish immigrants and laborers, which was a compound of economic insecurity, xenophobia, and the kind of authoritarianism discussed by S. M. Lipset in *Political Man* (Chapter 4), there was widespread resentment of the

Parnellites and their tactics among the middle and upper classes in England. One example out of many was A. J. Mundella's attack on the Parnellites in a letter to H. J. Wilson in 1881. Mundella, who was considered a Radical, accused some of the Irish members of dishonesty and declared he would rather have the Tories in office for the rest of his life than see Ireland at the mercy of the Parnellites. See W. S. Fowler, *A Study in Radicalism and Dissent* (London, 1961), pp. 66-72.

14. *Hansard,* 19, p. 49. Quoted in J. H. Hexter, "The Protestant Revival and the Catholic Question in England, 1778-1829," *Jo. Modern History,* 8 (Sept., 1936), pp. 316-17.

15. *Hansard,* 3 S, 32, p. 735.

16. *Ibid.,* 4 S, 11, p. 41.

17. Quoted in Richard Hofstadter, *Social Darwinism in American Thought* (Philadelphia, 1945), p. 146.

18. For a brief discussion of the rise of ethnological and anthropological societies in Great Britain, see G. Lienhardt, *Social Anthropology* (London, 1964), pp. 1-14, and J. W. Burrow, *Evolution and Society* (Cambridge, 1966), pp. 118-36.

19. For the background to that reunion in the early 1870's see, besides the work by Burrow, the presidential address of Arthur Keith, "How Can the Institute Best Serve the Needs of Anthropology?" *Jo. Royal Anthropological Institute,* 47 (1917), pp. 12-30.

20. Sidonia went on to explain to his audience of Young Englishmen that civilizations declined because the race was "worn out." "The decay of a race," he concluded, 'is an inevitable necessity, unless it lives in the deserts and never mixes its blood." *Tancred* (London, 1887), pp. 148-50. H. S. Chamberlain must have had this passage in mind when he referred to Sidonia's *obiter dicta* on race in *The Foundations of the Nineteenth Century* (London, 1911), I, p. 271. He not only garbled the quotation but assigned it incorrectly to *Coningsby*. This latter work contains some revealing Sidonian aphorisms on the importance of Jewish racial purity. See *Coningsby* (Nelson edition, n.d.), pp. 235-36 and 268-69. There is a succinct discussion of Disraeli's views on racial purity in Robert Blake, *Disraeli* (London, 1966), pp. 202-05.

21. These cells were called gemmules, and they were, according to the doctrine of pangenesis, supposed to transmit all the important traits from parent to child. See L. Eiseley, *Darwin's Century* (New York, 1958), pp. 216-21, 224-25.

22. See S. Kliger, *The Goths in England* (Cambridge, Mass., 1952) and the criticism of his treatment of the Levellers in C. Hill, "The Norman Yoke," *op. cit.,* p. 80, n. 1.

23. For an illuminating discourse on the legal and juridical mythology which enveloped the constitution in the late sixteenth and seventeenth centuries, see J. G. A. Pocock, *The Ancient Constitution and the Feudal Law* (Cambridge, 1957), Chapters 1-3.

24. Throughout most of the eighteenth century the word Goth was often used to connote "one who behaves like a barbarian . . . a rude, uncivilized, or ignorant person; one devoid of culture and taste." 'Gothicism' first meant "rudeness, barbarism." *Oxford English Dictionary* (1933), IV, pp. 312-13.

25. Some idea of the tone may be gauged from the following editorial invocation to Anglo-Saxon unity and achievement: "The whole earth may be called the *Father-land* of the Anglo-Saxon. He is a native of every clime, a messenger of heaven to every worker of this Planet; not indeed yet developed to his perfection, not yet even comprehending his mission, but *tending thitherward;* he runs to and fro upon the Earth's surface, accumulates facts, lays up in store the treasures and discoveries of every zone, and records, ever records, the results of his enterprize and experience, and investigations, in his own *Mother Tongue." The Anglo-Saxon*, I (Jan., 1848) 1, p. 4.

26. The life span of Anglo-Saxonist journals and reviews was much shorter than that of Celticist journals. Not only did *The Anglo-Saxon* disappear after one year of publication in 1849, but *The Anglo-Saxon Review*, an even more lavish production launched by Lady Randolph Churchill in June, 1899, survived for no more than ten numbers, dying in 1901. With poets like Tennyson and Alfred Austin and novelists like Kingsley and Lytton writing in an overtly Anglo-Saxonist vein, there was less need for such blatantly ethnocentric as well as expensive journals in England. For allusions to some of the Celticist journals in the second half of the century, see *infra*. pp. 112-13, 146-47.

27. The argument that English impressions of the West African reality underwent a double distortion as a result of the "culture filters" worn both by those Englishmen who visited the region and those who read what the former had to say about their experiences may be found in P. D. Curtin, *op. cit.* See esp. pp. 479-80.

28. An example of this rare type may be found in *The Irish Peasant, A Sociological Study*, "By a Guardian of the Poor" (London, 1892). The author of this revealing work, a "university educated" Anglo-Irishman, lived for two years among his tenants and then walked across the country dressed as a mason. He found that the "more primitive and less civilised Irish were the best mannered" and that those Irishmen who had been to England or America were generally rude and offensive. Like most Anglo-Saxonists he equated differences of race in Ireland with those of religion. See *ibid.*, pp. 18 f.

Chapter III

1. There were, of course, some exceptions to this pattern. Grant Allen, that prolific intellectual nonconformist, argued that Celtic blood preponderated in the British Isles. George Meredith did not go so far as this, but he acknowledged the "large admixture" of Celtic blood in the English people. These were the views of a small, and at times unpopular, minority. See C. G. Allen, "Are We Englishmen?" *Fortnightly Review*, 28 NS (Oct., 1880), pp. 472-87, and *Letters of George Meredith*, ed. by his son (London, 1912), I, p. 322.

2. For a thoughtful discussion of earlier theories in England about the varieties of man and the nature of savages, see M. T. Hodgen, *Early Anthropology in the Sixteenth and Seventeenth Centuries* (Philadelphia, 1964).

3. Michelet appreciated the mixture of races in the French people but believed that the original inhabitants were Gaelic: "La base originaire, celle qui a tout reçu, tout accepté, c'est cette jeune, molle et mobile race des Gaels, bruyante, sensuelle et légère, prompte à apprendre, prompte à dedaigner, avide de choses nouvelles. Voilà l'élément primitif, l'élément perfectible." J. Michelet, *Histoire de France* (Paris, 1835), I, p. 129.

4. The edition used here is the English translation by Adrian Collins (London, 1915).

5. *Ibid.*, pp. 29-31, 179. Gobineau was more than ambiguous on the subject of racial purity and national survival. Any race, he argued, that retained its original biological elements would never die; not even war could destroy the life of a nation so long as its blood remained unsullied by that of other races. And yet Gobineau stated that all conquest tended to the mixture of races, and the more powerful and expansionist a nation, the more rapidly did its racial character change as its blood became mixed with that of conquered peoples. See *ibid.*, pp. 1-34, 134-40. My own reading of Gobineau has been much enhanced by M. D. Biddiss' article, "Gobineau and the Origins of European Racism," *Race*, 7 (Jan., 1966), 3, pp. 255-70.

6. Gobineau contended that all great civilizations derived from the white races and that a society is "great and brilliant only so far as it preserves the blood of the noble group that created it, provided that this group belongs to the most illustrious branch of our species." *Op. cit.*, p. 210.

7. By Celts Renan meant four major groups of families who were juxtaposed to the Teutons and neo-Latins. These were the Welsh and Cornish peoples, the Bretons of Brittany, the Gaels of northwestern Scotland, and the Irish. Renan thought that the secret of Ireland's "irremediable weak-

ness" might lie in the fact that it was the only country in Europe where the natives could produce pedigrees dating back to the "darkness of prehistoric ages." *The Poetry of the Celtic Races* (London, 1896), translated by W. G. Hutchison, p. 4.

8. *Ibid.*, p. 8.

9. *Ibid.*, p. 14.

10. For two helpful studies of this work see R. Bromwich, *Matthew Arnold and Celtic Literature* (Oxford, 1965), and F. E. Faverty, *Matthew Arnold, the Ethnologist* (Evanston, 1951).

11. The most perceptive exposure of the literary sources and consequences of Arnold's essay is John V. Kelleher, "Matthew Arnold and the Celtic Revival," in *Perspectives of Criticism*, ed. Harry Levin (Cambridge, Mass., 1950), pp. 197-221.

12. See Faverty, *op. cit.*, pp. 117-18. As Arnold recalled, his father "never wearied" of contrasting the two races, relying heavily on Lord Lyndhurst's purported description of the Irish as "aliens in speech, in religion, in blood."

13. Arnold was reminded by some of his relatives of the Celtic blood in his veins, and he subsequently speculated about the influence of Cornish and Irish ancestors on the maternal side of his family. See *ibid.*, pp. 116-17.

14. Arnold, *On the Study of Celtic Literature* (London, Everyman edition), pp. 78-79.

15. *Ibid.*, pp. 80-81.

16. "The skillful and resolute appliance of means to ends which is needed both to make progress in material civilisation and also to form powerful states, is just what the Celt has least turn for." *Ibid.*, p. 84.

17. *Ibid.*, p. 136.

18. See Arnold's *Irish Essays* (London, 1882) and especially "The Incompatibles," pp. 1-81; and his two letters to the *Times* in 1886 reprinted in *On Home Rule for Ireland* (London, 1891).

19. C. Dilke, *Greater Britain: A Record of Travel in English-Speaking Countries During 1866 and 1867.* (Philadelphia, 1869), 2 vols. in 1.

20. *Ibid.*, II, p. 345.

21. *Ibid.*, I, pp. 36-41, 226, 259-60; II, pp. 346-47.

22. *Ibid.*, I, p. 109.

23. *Ibid.*, p. 226.

24. *Ibid.*, pp. 259-60. Like Gobineau Dilke was not at all consistent about the effects of miscegenation or about the purity of the Irish race in America. He argued that the assimilation of the Irish in America transformed the "son of Fenian Pat and bright-eyed Biddy" into the "normal, gaunt American . . . whom we have begun to recognize as the latest produce of the Saxon race." See *ibid.*, pp. 109, 113, 236, 260-62.

25. *Ibid.*, p. 268.

26. *Edinburgh Review*, 84 (Oct., 1846), 170, p. 267.

27. *Quarterly Review*, 126 (Jan., 1869), 251, p. 78.

28. See for example *ibid.*, 151 (Jan., 1881), 301, pp. 260-61.

Chapter IV

1. *The Works of John Ruskin* (London, 1908), vol. 36, p. 383.

2. Quoted in A. H. Hardinge, *The Life of . . . Carnarvon* (London, 1925), III, p. 196.

3. W. H. Long to M. Nathan, 21 April 1915, Nathan MS 455, f. 273.

4. Quoted in Robert Blake, *op. cit.*, p. 131.

5. E. W. T. Hamilton to Edward Hamilton, 30 Oct. 1873, Hamilton Papers, Add. Ms 48620, packet 11.

6. E. W. T. Hamilton to Edward Hamilton, 19 Nov. 1878, *ibid.* I am indebted to Prof. Dudley Bahlman for this and the preceding reference.

7. Quoted in J. Lehmann, *All Sir Garnet* (London, 1964), p. 24. Another general who thought he knew something about Ireland was Kitchener, who declared after the Easter rising that he did not trust "one single Irishman with a rifle in his hand one single yard." See J. R. White, *Misfit* (London, 1930), p. 335.

8. Although the word 'Paddy' was presumably in use at an earlier date, the *Oxford English Dictionary* cites as the first significant use of this abbreviation of the name Padraig or Patrick the following passage from Arthur Young's *A Tour in Ireland* (Dublin, 1780), I, p. 28: "The paddies were swimming their horses in the sea to cure the mange, or keep them in health." The word came into much wider circulation in England during the first half of the nineteenth century. Disraeli wrote that "Paddy was tripped up" in his novel *Vivian Gray* (London, 1826). The word was also

used in the sense of 'bamboozling or humbugging' someone. Another common term for an Irishman was 'Paddywhack' which also meant a rage, passion, or temper.

9. For a treatment of the "stage Irishman" in England, especially in the seventeenth and eighteenth centuries, see G. C. Duggan, *The Stage Irishman* (London, 1937) and J. O. Bartley, *Teague, Shenkin, and Sawney* (Cork, 1954). The best work on Irish bulls, those undefinable and witty "incongruities" of thought and speech, is, of course, Richard and Maria Edgeworth, *Essay on Irish Bulls* (London, 1803), 2nd edn. The literature of Paddy lore in England is voluminous. Some of the better examples of this genre are: Baron de Mandat-Grancey, *Paddy At Home* (London, 1889), 5th edn., *Irish Jests and Anecdotes: Nuggets for Travellers*, anon. (London, 1895), Andrew Merry, *Paddy Risky: Irish Realities of Today* (London, 1903), and *Real Life in Ireland* "by a Real Paddy," (London, 1904).

10. These meanings are taken from A. A. Roback, *A Dictionary of International Slurs* (Cambridge, Mass., 1944), pp. 21-69.

11. Among the most common virtues or assets attributed to Irishmen were a capacity for hard work and suffering, a remarkable sense of humor and native wit as expressed in 'bulls,' courage in war, shrewdness in driving a bargain, and adherence to a relatively strict sexual morality. The incompatibility of some of these virtues with the vices assigned to the same people did not, of course, deter Englishmen from accepting the stereotype of Paddy without hesitation.

12. "A Week in the West of Ireland," *National Review*, 46 (Sept., 1905), 271, p. 77.

13. W. H. Long to M. Nathan, 18 Dec. 1914, Nathan MS 455, ff. 224.

14. Countess of Leitrim to Nathan, 30 March 1915, *ibid.*, f. 212-15.

15. As Lord Salisbury intimated to Sir Michael Hicks Beach on 28 Feb. 1887, Salisbury MS.

16. For an analysis of the interaction of continence in both sexual and economic activity among the respectable 'Christian gentlemen' of Victorian England, see P. T. Cominos' article in *International Review of Social History*, VIII (1963), parts I and II. The stereotypical Irish Celt represented the exact antithesis of the Victorian ideal of the manly, continent gentleman in all respects save the important area of sexual restraint or inhibition. Samuel Smiles' portraits of industrialists and political as well as spiritual leaders in such works as *Self-help, Duty, Character*, and *Thrift* might be described as 'profiles in continence.' His paragons were men of self-discipline and self-control.

17. *Edinburgh Review,* 59 (April, 1834), 119, p. 235.

18. *Ibid.,* 96 (Oct., 1852), 196, p. 400.

19. *Ibid.,* 127 (April, 1868), 260, p. 503.

20. "Race and Life on English Soil," *Fraser's Magazine,* 26 NS (Sept., 1882), 153, p. 319.

21. *Tales of Irish Life and Character* (London, 1909), pp. 24, 191-92, 208-209.

22. "The Unionist Reaction," *Quarterly Review,* 176 (April, 1893), 352, p. 563.

23. In *Lord Kilgobbin* (London, 1906), pp. 6-7, Lever wrote with some exaggeration that the word 'evicted' might have been a surgical operation for all the peasantry knew about it. This analogy was unfortunately more apt than he knew.

24. See D. B. Quinn, *op. cit.,* pp. 39, 65, 76-77. Lithgow observed: "True it is, to make a fit comparison, that the barbarian Moor, the Moorish Spaniard, the Turk, and the Irishman are the least industrious and most sluggish livers under the sun." Quoted in "Tours in Ireland," *Quarterly Review,* 85 (Sept., 1849), 170, p. 499.

25. *Ibid.*

26. Young described the Irish as "Hard drinkers and quarrelsome; great liars, but civil, submissive and obedient." He divided the Irish people into three races: the Spanish in Kerry and in parts of Limerick and Cork, the Scotch in the north, and "mongrels," chiefly Milesian, scattered over the rest of the country. A. Young, *A Tour in Ireland* (Dublin, 1780), II, pp. 106-07.

27. Quoted in *Quarterly Review,* 85 (Sept., 1849), 170, p. 502.

28. *Ibid.,* pp. 518-19.

29. Bishop Doyle thus wrote in his pastoral letter on tithes in 1832: "Your situation never can or will improve until unceasing industry succeed to idleness." Quoted in *Edinburgh Review,* 79 (Jan., 1844), 159, p. 209.

30. See for example S. C. Hall's classic account of Irish cabin life in his *Retrospect of a Long Life* (New York, 1883), pp. 482-83.

31. For Carlyle's indictment of the conditions endured by Irishmen in Ireland and Britain see Chapter 4 in his essay on Chartism: *The Works of Thomas Carlyle* (London, 1899), vol. 29, pp. 134-44. Carlyle's vivid description of Irishmen with their "wild Milesian features, looking false ingenuity, restlessness, unreason, misery and mockery" reveals some of his

own ambivalence about Irish Celts. The Prussian tourist, Friedrich von Raumer, wrote that the squalor and misery he had seen in Ireland during 1835 made it "the most melancholy" experience of his life. See his *England in 1835* (London, 1836), I, pp. 464-65.

32. "It is to me incredible that the greediest *pigs* on record — the *Irish* Unionist pig — should be content not to have his feet, or some one of them, in the *Trough*." A. Birrell to M. Nathan, Whit Monday 1915, Nathan MS 449, f. 181. See also A. Birrell to M. Nathan, 4 Nov. 1914, *ibid.*, ff. 21-22. Not all Englishmen regarded the Irish as pigs. Colonel Thomas Sandys, M. P. for Lancashire, S. W., Bootle, caused an uproar in an election address in 1886 by referring to the Irish as "savage dogs" who ought to be tied up and then throttled. There were always Englishmen who preferred the feline image as contained in the story of the Kilkenny cats who fought so viciously that only their tails were left behind.

33. See Sir Harry Johnston's description of Neanderthaloid or neolithic archetypes in Ireland in *Views and Reviews* (London, 1912), pp. 62-73.

34. Horace Plunkett Diary, M. Digby typescript, Plunkett House, pp. 64, 75.

35. *The Life and Letters of . . . F. Max Müller*, edited by his wife (London, 1902), II, p. 253.

36. *Descent of Man* (Modern Library edition), pp. 544-45. For Kingsley's use of the same analogy, see *infra*. p. 140.

37. *Times*, 27 March 1893.

38. See especially the gruesome pictures of Irish Fenians and assassins drawn by Sir John Tenniel in *Mr. Punch's Victorian Era* (London, 1887), pp. 23, 122, 151, 179, 206; and compare these physiognomies with those of loyalist Irishmen being sworn in as deputy constables during the Fenian troubles in 1868 on p. 161. In W. H. Maxwell's *History of the Irish Rebellion in 1798* (London, 1845), the Irish rebels are portrayed with the same apelike, brutal features. See also Erskine Nicol's dramatic portrait of a wild, disorderly Irishman with shillelagh poised on high which he called simply and graphically "Home Rule" — reproduced in Mrs. S. C. Hall, *Tales of Irish Life and Character* (London, 1909), facing p. 24.

39. *Edinburgh Review*, 79 (Jan., 1844), 159, pp. 198, 203. The criminal habits of the Irish in Britain caused much concern. According to one estimate in 1868 the Irish comprised one-thirtieth of the total population of England and Wales and yet made up one-fifth of all prisoners in jail. And in Scotland where the Irish constituted one-fifteenth of the population, they accounted for one-fourth of all prisoners. *Ibid.*, 127 (April, 1868), 260, p. 526. For an amusing example of English literature about Irish rowdiness, see the account of a 'shindy' on board a boat plying between

Liverpool and Dublin in *Paddiana* (London, 1847), anon. The attribution of violence had considerable documentation behind it. The word atrocity may well be applied to some of the crimes committed in Ireland from the Dillon, Lawrence, and Connell cases in 1813 to the Maamtrasna murders in 1881. See N. Gash, *Mr. Secretary Peel* (London, 1961), pp. 167-80. Whether these crimes were any more atrocious than some of those committed in London or the English provinces is, of course, another matter.

40. "The Celt is thus peculiarly disposed to feel the spell of the feminine idiosyncracy; he has an affinity to it; he is not far from its secret." Arnold, *op. cit.*, 86.

41. See "Ulster and its People," *Fraser's Magazine*, 14 NS (Aug. 1876), 80, p. 221.

42. Lady Gregory Diary, 24 Aug. 1882, Gregory MS, New York Public Library.

43. Quoted in M. Digby, *Horace Plunkett* (Oxford, 1949), p. 91.

44. G. Myrdal, *An American Dilemma* (New York, 1962). See Appendix 5, "A Parallel to the Negro Problem," pp. 1073-78, and also pp. 67 n., 103.

45. "[The Irish] . . . are usually most successful where the framework of society is Anglo-Saxon. . . . They possess, no doubt, qualities of a very serviceable kind, but these qualities require the example and the power of another race, more highly endowed, to bring them to perfection and turn them to full account. . . . The Irish are deficient in that unquiet energy, that talent for accumulation, those indefinite desires, which are the mainsprings of successful colonisation, and they are deficient too in that faculty of self-government without which free institutions can neither flourish nor be permanently maintained." "The Irish Abroad," *Edinburgh Review*, 127 (April, 1868), 260, p. 507.

46. S. C. Hall, *op. cit.*, p. 511.

47. This quotation is also of interest because Sidney Webb wrote all of the letter to Wallas, dated 29 July 1892, except for the last ten words (italicized). Beatrice added those lethal words in her own hand; and her vehemence may be explained, in part, by her postscript to the letter: "We are very very happy — far too happy to be reasonable." Quoted in Janet Beveridge, *An Epic of Clare Market* (London, 1960), p. 9. For other examples of the Webbs' Anglo-Saxonism, see *Industrial Democracy* (London, 1902), pp. 3, 7, 22, 82-88, 744 n.1.

48. M. Digby, *op. cit.*, p. 92.

49. *Ibid.*, pp. 170-71.

50. *Ibid.*, pp. 164-65.

51. *Ibid.*, pp. 108-9, 278. See also his *Ireland in the New Century* (London, 1904). Plunkett wrote: ". . . in the last analysis the problem of Irish ineffectiveness at home is in the main a problem of character — and of Irish character." *Ibid.*, p. 32.

52. Gordon Allport has defined projection as "the tendency to attribute falsely to other people motives or traits that are our own, or that in some way explain or justify our own." Allport, *op. cit.*, p. 382. His attempt to distinguish three types of projection does not illuminate the Irish situation wherein such compartments as 'direct,' 'mote-beam,' and 'complementary' projection cannot be neatly isolated. See *ibid.*, pp. 382-91. The classic case of extreme projection may be found in Sigmund Freud's "Psycho-analytic Notes on an Autobiographical Account of a Case of Paranoia (Dementia Paranoides)" in James Strachey, ed., *The Standard Edition of the Complete . . . Works* (London, 1958), XII, pp. 9-82. Needless to say, I am not suggesting that Anglo-Saxonists suffered from the same acute symptoms as Dr. D. P. Schreber. The word is used here in a more general-ized sense to explain the mechanism by which persons defend themselves against their own unpleasant thoughts and fantasies. Freud recognized the broader applicability of this term, but there are a few other references to projection in his published works.

53. See for example Henry V. Dicks, "Personality Traits and National Socialist Ideology," *Human Relations*, 3 (1950), 2, pp. 112-43; D. J. Levin-son and R. N. Sanford, "A Scale for the Measurement of Anti-Semitism," *Jo. of Psychology*, 17 (1944), pp. 339-70; and E. Frenkel-Brunswick and R. N. Sanford, "Some Personality Factors in Anti-Semitism," *Ibid.*, 20 (1945), pp. 271-91. The role of projection in shaping the Anglo-Saxonist stereotype of Paddy did not, of course preclude the presence of a residue of reality in some of the traits ascribed to Irishmen; but that residue was distorted out of all proportion in order to fulfill the needs of those who ac-cepted the stereotype.

54. G. Myrdal, *op. cit.*, p. 669.

Chapter V

1. The definitive history of anthropology and ethnology in Great Britain has yet to be written, but some of the foundations, however porous in places, have been laid by T. K. Penniman, *A Hundred Years of Anthro-pology* (London, 1935), G. Lienhardt, *op. cit.*, and J. W. Burrow, *op. cit.*

2. In addition to the above works, and the writings of the men in ques-tion, see H. E. Hutchinson, *Life of Sir John Lubbock, Lord Avebury* (Lon-

don, 1914), 2 vols., and for a study of Prichard, see D. Leigh, *The Historical Development of British Psychiatry* (London, 1961), I, pp. 148-209.

3. William Stanton's *The Leopard's Spots* (Chicago, 1966) contains a fascinating account of the careers and theories of Gliddon, Nott, and Morton.

4. T. H. Huxley, "On the Methods and Results of Ethnology," *Fortnightly Review,* I (1865), p. 257. See also J. C. Prichard's definition of ethnology in "On the Relations of Ethnology to Other Branches of Knowledge," *Jo. Ethnological Society,* I (1848), pp. 301-29.

5. D. Mackintosh, "The Comparative Anthropology of England and Wales," *Anthropological Review and Journal,* hereafter *ARJ,* IV (Jan., 1866), p. 1.

6. *Ibid.,* V (1867), pp. xliv-lxx, 17.

7. R. Knox, *The Races of Man, A Fragment* (London, 1850), pp. 2-6, 11, 323-29, 346-50.

8. *Ibid.,* pp. 6, 19, 26-27.

9. D. Mackintosh, "The Comparative Anthropology of England and Wales," *ARJ,* IV (1866), pp. 1-15, 16.

10. *Ibid.,* p. 17.

11. For details of Beddoe's career see his *Memories of Eighty Years* (London, 1910), *DNB, 1901-1911* (London, 1912), pp. 124-25, and T. K. Penniman, *op. cit.,* pp. 110-11.

12. Beddoe's index of nigrescence was based on five categories of hair and eye color ranging from light to dark. To arrive at the gross index he weighted the 'black factor' by doubling it in his equation. The index was supposed to establish the residual amount of so-called 'Africanoid' elements in the population. J. Beddoe, *The Races of Britain* (London, 1885), pp. 2-8, 268. According to Beddoe, "It was the ancient controversy respecting the colour of the hair of the Kelts, then burning briskly enough, and even now still smouldering, that led me to begin systematic numerical observations in physical anthropology." *Ibid.,* p. 2.

13. *ARJ,* V (1867), p. 20.

14. J. Beddoe, *op. cit.,* pp. 10-11. According to the "German Method" of calculating "racial colour-types" Ireland had an index of nigrescence of 65 percent, compared with 28 percent for the Bristol area, 60 percent for Wales, and 41 percent for the Scottish Highlands, pp. 219-20. Beddoe also published in this remarkable book the results of thousands of morphological observations made across Western Europe.

15. Beddoe believed in the "prevalent idea" that the English people were "gradually changing from a fair to a dark race, while the sanguine is giving place to the nervous or nervo-bilious temperament," although he admitted that this belief rested on speculation rather than sound evidence. He went on to suggest that there were positive connections between fair complexions and good health as well as athletic prowess and that, with a few exceptions, the "conquering and ruling races have always been fair, while the vanquished and submissive races have been dark. The supposed superiority in stature is . . . an affair of races, rather than of individuals." *Ibid.*, pp. 223-24. For Beddoe's allusion to the connection between intelligence and 'long-headed blonds,' based on a study of first-class men at Cambridge carried out by Dr. Venn, see his *The Anthropological History of Europe* (Paisley, 1912), p. 185.

16. To paraphrase Robert W. Gibbes's remark, quoted in W. Stanton, *op. cit.*, p. 144. It is worth noting that the number of articles specifically devoted to Ireland and Irishmen in the *Journal of the Anthropological Institute* fell off markedly after 1880. Whereas there were some thirteen such articles published in the 1870's, only eight appeared in the years 1880-1897, and one of these was concerned also with England and Scotland. From 1871 to 1897 far more articles were devoted to Australasia, Asia, India, and Africa, as well as to methodology, than to Ireland or North America.

Chapter VI

1. General and somewhat dated introductions to English historiography in the nineteenth century are contained in G. P. Gooch, *History and Historians in the Nineteenth Century* (Boston, 1959), Chapters XIV-XIX, and Sir A. W. Ward, "Historians, Biographers and Political Orators" in *The Cambridge History of English Literature*, (New York, 1933), XIV, Part III, pp. 55-116.

2. See Gooch, *op. cit.*, Chapters II-VIII. Most of these English historians had good friends among the ranking German historians of their day. To say that they were much impressed by the standards of German historiography does not, of course, mean that they were uncritical of the writings of men like Niebuhr, Mommsen, or Ihne.

3. S. Turner, *The History of the Anglo-Saxons* (London, 1852), 7th edn., III, pp. 1-2.

4. Geoffrey Keating, *The History of Ireland*, ed. David Comyn for Irish Texts Society (London, 1902), I, p. 77. Keating's refutation of those writers who had debased the Irish people from Bede and Giraldus to Stany-

hurst, Moryson, and Davies should be read by all students of Anglo-Irish relations. *Ibid.*, pp. 1-95.

5. Lord Macaulay, *The History of England* (New York, 1849), I, p. 61. For some of Macaulay's private reflections on Ireland, see Sir G. O. Trevelyan, *The Life and Letters of Lord Macaulay* (New York, 1909), II, pp. 227-30.

6. Apart from Gooch, *op. cit.*, pp. 27-72 and the *DNB*, X, pp. 1257-60, there are some reminiscences by his sister, Frances A. Kemble, *Records of a Girlhood* (New York, 1884) 2nd edn., and an obituary in *Fraser's Magazine*, LV, (1857), pp. 612-18.

7. For useful discussions of the mark or march see *Encyclopedia Britannica*, 11th edn. (Cambridge, 1910-11), XVII, pp. 688-89, 728, and W. J. Ashley, *Surveys Historic and Economic* (London, 1900), pp. 39-60, 161-66.

8. See G. L. von Maurer's classic works, *Geschichte der Markenverfassung in Deutschland* (1856) and *Geschichte der Stadtverfassung in Deutschland* (1869-71). Stubbs called Maurer "the great authority" on the mark system in his *The Constitutional History of England* (Oxford, 1926), I, p. 53, n. 1.

9. F. de Coulanges, *The Origin of Property in Land* (London, 1892, 2nd edn.), trans. by Margaret Ashley with an introduction by W. J. Ashley, "The English Manor," pp. vii-xlviii; and Charles M. Andrews, *The Old English Manor* (Baltimore, 1892). See esp. Andrews' introduction, pp. 1-81.

10. Kemble dedicated his book, *The Saxons in England* (London, 1876, 2nd edn.), to the Queen because his was a history of "the principles which have given her empire its preeminence among the nations of Europe." For Kemble's discussion of the mark see *ibid.*, I, pp. 35-71.

11. For biographical details of Freeman see W. R. W. Stephens, *The Life and Letters of Edward A. Freeman* (London, 1895), 2 vols. and *DNB Supplement*, XXII, pp. 672-76. The first three lectures in *Comparative Politics* (London, 1873) are most relevant to the Anglo-Saxonist theme.

12. W. Stephens, *op. cit.*, I, p. 115.

13. *Ibid.*, pp. 294-300. Freeman was in the habit of referring to Schleswig as "Old England." His pronounced Germanophilia erupted at the time of the Franco-Prussian war. *Ibid.*, II, pp. 2-11.

14. *Ibid.*, p. 242. Freeman was not satisfied by calling Negroes "niggers"; he preferred to describe them as "big monkeys dressed up for a game," and he was distressed by the thought that in America "one of these great black apes may (in theory) be President." *Ibid.*, pp. 234, 236.

15. *Ibid.*, pp. 177-84. For an account of this memorable trip, see "Mr. Freeman's Visit to Baltimore" by the editor (Herbert B. Adams), in *Johns Hopkins University Studies in Historical and Political Science*, hereafter *JHUS* (Baltimore, 1883), I, pp. 5-12.

16. *Manchester Guardian*, 23 March 1892. The author was J. Earle. J. Bryce, "Edward Augustus Freeman," *English Historical Review*, 7 (July, 1892), 27, pp. 497-509.

17. Freeman to Bryce, 2 May 1886, Bryce MS 7, f. 219. On May 8, Freeman wrote again: "Do keep out the Paddies, if you can. I don't ever see how they can be let in. But I should still fight for the Bill, though thinking it sadly spoiled." *Ibid.*, f. 223. For Freeman's warnings about the dangers of carrying racialist doctrines too far, see his "Race and Language," *Contemporary Review*, 29 (March, 1877), pp. 711-41.

18. William Stubbs, *op. cit.*, I, p. 2. For Stubbs's sympathetic views on the mark system see pp. 52-58. Another Oxford man who popularized the 'Germanic origins' thesis was Thomas Pitt Taswell-Langmead in his *English Constitutional History . . .* (London, 1890, 4th edn.), pp. 1-12.

19. Quoted in W. H. Hutton, ed., *The Letters of William Stubbs* (London, 1904), pp. 185-86.

20. Leslie Stephen, ed., *The Letters of John Richard Green* (New York, 1901), pp. 24, 28, 37, 91.

21. *A Short History of the English People* (London, 1902), I, pp. 308-09, 1-7, 23-26.

22. In an important letter to James Bryce on 1 Nov. 1882, Dicey wrote: "Godkin assumes an amount of *available* Irish political capacity which I fear does not at the present moment exist." Bryce MS 2, f. 40-43. Several years later Dicey wrote to Bryce: "I firmly believe that under the Continental system Ireland might be well and happily governed." 4 Jan. 1885, *ibid.*, ff. 69-73. See also Dicey to Bryce, 25 Dec. 1901, *ibid.* 3, ff. 7-8. Dicey served as an unofficial but effective spokesman for the Unionist coalition on the question of Home Rule. His closely reasoned contribution to the Unionist cause in 1893 was *A Leap in the Dark* (London, 1911, 2nd edn.).

23. Goldwin Smith, *Irish History and Irish Character* (Oxford, 1861), pp. 3-6, 10-12, 18-19. See also Elisabeth Wallace, *Goldwin Smith, Victorian Liberal* (Toronto, 1957).

24. (London, 1875). See the preface by F. Max Müller. Kingsley took as his major theme "the assault of our Teutonic race on Rome." Unlike most other Anglo-Saxonists he emphasized the "childishness" of England's Teutonic ancestors. Kingsley's chapter on "The Forest Children" assumes significance when one compares this piece of fantasy with the curious reality

set forth in John Johnson's essay, *Rudimentary Society Among Boys* in *JHUS,* II (Baltimore, 1884), XI. See *infra.* pp. 96, 142.

25. *Charles Kingsley, His Letters and Memories of His Life,* ed. by his Wife (London, 1877), II, p. 107. In *Hereward the Wake,* a classic example of fictional ethnology, Kingsley wrote, in words reminiscent of Darwin: "The Irish were desperately brave. . . . Ill-armed and almost naked, they were as perfect in the arts of forest warfare as those modern Maories whom they so much resembled." (Everyman edition, London, 1935), p. 73.

26. For details of Froude's Oxford career as a young man see W. H. Dunn, *James Anthony Froude* (Oxford, 1961), I, pp. 47-61, 72-121. His sojourn with the family of the Rev. William Cleaver in county Wicklow is described in *ibid.,* pp. 62-68.

27. *Ibid.,* I, pp. 68-69.

28. This novel or "Irish romance" was published in 1889. See *ibid.,* II, pp. 558-60.

29. *The Two Chiefs of Dunboy* (London, 1891, New edn.), pp. 156-57.

30. *History of England from the Fall of Wolsey to the Death of Elizabeth* (New York, 1881), II, pp. 245-47. Froude was at heart an imperial unionist who enunciated his faith in the unity of the empire in *Oceana, England and Her Colonies* (New York, 1886).

31. *The English in Ireland in the Eighteenth Century* (London, 1895), I, pp. 11-12. "There is no disputing against strength, nor happily is there need to dispute, for the strength which gives a right to freedom, implies the presence of those qualities which ensure that it will be rightly used." *Ibid.,* p. 12.

32. *Ibid.,* III, p. 558. Froude believed that the Irish suffered from an "incompleteness of character" and above all from an excess of passion. His image of the Irish deserves attention: "Light-hearted, humorous, imaginative, susceptible through the entire range of feeling, from the profoundest pathos to the most playful jest, if they possess some real virtues they possess the counterfeits of a hundred more. Passionate in everything — passionate in their patriotism, passionate in their religion, passionately courageous, passionately loyal and affectionate — they are without the manliness which will give strength and solidity to the sentimental part of their dispositions; while the surface and show is so seductive and so winning that only experience of its instability can resist the charm." *Ibid.,* I, pp. 22-23.

33. "Mr. Froude's English in Ireland," *Macmillan's Magazine,* 27 (Jan., 1873), pp. 246-64, and 30 (June, 1874), pp. 166-84.

34. J. A. Froude, "Romanism and the Irish Race," *North American Review,* Part I, 129 (Dec., 1879), 277, p. 523, and Part II, 130 (Jan., 1880),

280. This article was rebutted by the Roman Catholic Bishop of Peoria in a scathing reply, called "Mr. Froude's Historical Method," *ibid.*, 130 (March, 1880), 280, pp. 280-99.

35. Among the best available sources for Lecky's life and its relation to his writings are: Mrs. Elisabeth Lecky, *A Memoir of the Rt. Hon. William E. H. Lecky* (New York, 1910), 2nd edn.; J. J. Auchmuty, *Lecky* (Dublin, 1945); Miss Helen Mulvey, "The Historian Lecky: Opponent of Irish Home Rule," *Victorian Studies*, I, (June, 1958), pp. 337-51; and D. Mc-Cartney, "Lecky's Leaders of Public Opinion in Ireland," *Irish Historical Studies*, XIV (1964), pp. 119-41.

36. E. Lecky, *op. cit.*, p. 158.

37. W. E. H. Lecky, *History of European Morals from Augustus to Charlemagne* (London, 1911), p. 58.

38. Lecky, *A History of England in the Eighteenth Century* (London, 1882), IV, p. 560. See also Lecky's *The Leaders of Public Opinion in Ireland* (London, 1871), 2nd edn., esp. the chapters on Flood and Grattan.

39. Among Lecky's numerous published contributions to the Liberal Unionist cause are: letters to the *Times*, 13 Jan., 3 May, 7 June 1886; "A Nationalist Parliament," *Nineteenth Century*, XIX (April, 1886), pp. 636-44. "Ireland in the Light of History" and "Why Home Rule is Undesirable," *North American Review*, CLII (Jan., March, 1891), pp. 11-26, 349-70; and "Some Aspects of Home Rule," *Contemporary Review*, LXIII (May, 1893), pp. 626-38.

40. W. Lecky, *Democracy and Liberty* (London, 1896), 2 vols. See esp. I, pp. 138-75, 188-91, 358, and II, pp. 1-25.

41. E. Lecky, *op. cit.*, p. 169.

Chapter VII

1. Discussions of the 'German or Teutonic origins' thesis may be found in John Higham, *op. cit.*, Edward Saveth, *op. cit.*, and Barbara M. Solomon, *op. cit.* See esp. Mrs. Solomon's Chapters III and IV which bear directly on the attitudes of American Anglo-Saxonists towards the immigrant Irish. Oscar Handlin's well-known work, *Boston's Immigrants, 1790-1865* (Cambridge, Mass., 1941), pp. 67-70, 196-200, 206-21, contains revealing accounts of the prejudices encountered by working class Irish who crowded into the slums of Boston. Handlin makes the important connection between the "political mobilization" of the Irish, especially in the years 1845-55, and the rise of nativist hostility towards these people. See pp. 198 ff.

2. For the fears aroused in Anglo-Saxonists by the surge of Irish immigration, see anon., "The Anglo-Saxon Race," *North American Review,* LXXIII (July, 1851), pp. 34-71, and J. P. Bocock, "The Irish Conquest of Our Cities," *Forum,* XVII (April, 1894), pp. 186-95.

3. Herbert B. Adams acknowledged the Anglo-German (or Anglo-Saxon-Teutonic) sources of his inspiration in his famous essay, *The Germanic Origin of New England Towns,* JHUS I (Baltimore, 1882), II, pp. 10-11. See also Freeman's important "Introduction to American Institutional History," *ibid.,* pp. 13-39.

4. James K. Hosmer, *Samuel Adams, The Man of the Town-Meeting, ibid.,* II (Baltimore, 1884), IV, pp. 5-7.

5. *Ibid.,* p. 16.

6. For a more detailed discussion of these men see E. Saveth, *op. cit.,* Chapters 1-4 and B. Solomon, *op. cit.,* pp. 59-81, 234-38.

7. *Ibid.,* pp. 69-78.

8. See J. A. Banks, *Prosperity and Parenthood* (London, 1954), esp. Chapters 9-10.

9. J. Higham, *op. cit.,* p. 9.

10. Francis Parkman, *Representative Selections* (New York, 1938), pp. 380-82. This passage is quoted by Thomas F. Gosset in his comprehensive study of race thinking in America, *Race, the History of an Idea in America* (Dallas, 1963), p. 95.

11. John Johnson, *op. cit.,* JHUS, II (Baltimore, 1884), XI. Johnson began his fascinating essay with a quotation from Francis Galton: "Human nature is generally akin: . . . and the motives of an adult barbarian are very similar to those of a civilized child." Johnson's account of adolescent life in this artificially primitive society invites comparison with William Golding's *Lord of the Flies.*

12. See W. Stanton, *op. cit.* and T. F. Gossett, *op. cit.,* esp. Chapters 4-6, 13.

13. Aspects of that process of assimilation and acculturation are treated in O. Handlin, *op. cit.,* Carl Wittke, *The Irish in America* (Baton Rouge, 1956), William V. Shannon, *The American Irish* (New York, 1963), and Edward M. Levine, *The Irish and Irish Politicians* (Notre Dame, 1966).

Chapter VIII

1. No comprehensive study of these debates of 1886 and 1893-94 has yet been published. The arguments employed by both parties to the dispute deserve more attention from British domestic, as well as imperial, historians than they have hitherto received.

2. See the bound and indexed edition of Irish Unionist Alliance leaflets published in Dublin in 1893. A good example of this 'scare' literature is "How Nationalists Legislate," Leaflet No. 47, *IUA Publications* (Dublin, 1893), 6th Series, I, pp. 199-200. In Widener Library, Cambridge, Mass., there is a volume of Irish Loyal and Patriotic Union leaflets published in the 1880's which covers such topics as "How Boycotted People are Treated in Ireland: The Reign of Terror and Cruelty" (No. 5), "Begone, Saxon: Mr. T. M. Healy at Boston" (No. 7), "Outrages and Mutilation of Cattle in Ireland: The Last Galway Murder" (No. 40).

3. Take for example Lord Ashbourne's remarks in the House of Lords: "Who are the Irish people? Why more than one half of them are of English blood, a great many of them are of Scotch blood; there is a great intermixture of races in Ireland." *Hansard*, 3S, 306, p. 1280.

4. Chamberlain was only one of many Unionist spokesmen who alluded to the "bitter controversies" of race, class, religion, and party which had divided Ireland for years. The implication was that these sources of dissension were permanent features of the country. In August, 1893, the Duke of Abercorn declared in a speech that the Home Rule Bill proclaimed a "war of races, a war of classes, a war of creeds." *Annual Register, 1893*, p. 161.

5. Not all Gladstonian Liberals were environmentalists. Some buried their prejudices against Irishmen or the Parnellite party out of loyalty to Gladstone or ambition for office. Others like Bryce and Rosebery had second or third thoughts about the fitness of Irishmen for Home Rule. The number of safeguards in Gladstone's two bills show how qualified the environmentalist view of political equality for Irishmen could be.

6. *Hansard*, 3S, 304, pp. 1040, 1044-45, 1081, 1083.

7. *Ibid.*, p. 1540.

8. *Ibid.*, 306, p. 1163. In 1893 Goschen declared that "the Celtic races have never displayed that kind of cool patience and coolness of dealing which has always characterized the Parliaments of the Anglo-Saxon." *Ibid.*, 4S, 11, p. 468.

9. *Ibid.*, 3S, 304, p. 1267.

10. *Ibid.*, p. 1350.

11. *Ibid.*, pp. 1085-92.

12. *Ibid.*, pp. 1095-1104.

13. *Ibid.*, p. 1200. Chamberlain's Irish policies in the 1880's have yet to be placed by historians within the context of his overriding imperial ideology. The West Midlands context does not suffice in itself to explain his tortuous course between the Scylla of Parnellite Home Rule and the Charybdis of coercion. No one who has been through his papers at the University of Birmingham can fail to be impressed by the evidence of Chamberlain's interest in and knowledge of Irish affairs; but only the presence of Anglo-Saxonist prejudices can explain why he declared in December, 1885 that he would infinitely prefer "Separation" between England and Ireland to Tim Healy's unworkable Home Rule plan. But separation, he went on to assert, would lead to conscription in both Ireland and England, to an increase in the size of the fleet, to the fortification of the west coast of Scotland and England, and, finally, to war between the two countries with either America or France coming in on the side of the Irish. See Chamberlain to John Morley, 24 Dec. 1885, Chamberlain MS 5/54/669. Chamberlain was, of course, not alone in his dire prophecy about the likelihood of war following upon Home Rule. See Maj.-Gen. Sir Thomas Fraser, *The Military Danger of Home Rule for Ireland* (London, 1912).

14. *Hansard*, 3S, 304, pp. 1215-16.

15. *Ibid.*, p. 1395.

16. *Times*, 17 May 1886.

17. *Hansard*, 4S, 10, pp. 1597-1619. Summarizing the arguments against Home Rule, Gladstone said that according to his opponents, "The Irish, except in Ulster, have nothing human about them except the form. . . . All principles they trample under foot, all power that they get into their hands they will abuse. They have no sympathy with us, and they have not any operative or commanding sense of justice." *Ibid.*, p. 1603.

18. On this occasion Salisbury referred to the "native, constant, incurable differences and quarrelsomeness of the race." *Ibid.*, 4S, 11, p. 631.

19. Mommsen's description of both ancient Celts and modern Irish as "at all times and all places, the same indolent and poetical, irresolute and fervid, inquisitive, credulous, amiable, clever, but — in a political point of view — thoroughly useless nation" was a favorite among Anglo-Saxonists. See Theodor Mommsen, *The History of Rome* (London, 1894), V, pp. 98-100. For a blow-by-blow refutation of this charge against the Celts, see Robertson, *The Saxon and the Celt* (London, 1897), pp. 190-96, and Babington, *Fallacies of Race Theories* (London, 1895), pp. 181-92.

20. Babington, *op. cit.*, pp. 231-46.

21. Robertson, *op. cit.*, p. 63.

22. One Irishman who set out to smash the Anglo-Saxonist image of the Irish Celt was Edmond Hogan, S.J., in *The Irish People* (Dublin, 1899). Robert Dunlop, the historian of seventeenth century Ireland, tried to refute racialist arguments against the Irish in two articles in the *Quarterly Review*, CCV, (July, 1906), pp. 79-102, and CCX (Jan., 1909), pp. 254-75. Dunlop's own interpretation of Irish history was itself denounced as full of prejudice by that perennial defender of the Celticist faith, Alice Stopford Green in "Tradition in Irish History," *The Old Irish World* (Dublin, 1912), pp. 168-97. A lucid statement of the environmentalist position in Irish historiography may be found in Philip Wilson, *The Beginnings of Modern Ireland* (Dublin, 1912). See esp. his introduction, pp. 1-27.

23. See the debates in the House of Commons on Alien Immigration during 1904 and 1905 in *Hansard*, 4S, vols. 133 and 145 as well as Minutes of Evidence on Alien Immigration, *Parliamentary Papers, IX, Reports from Commissioners*, Cd. 1742. Anglo-Irish peers like Lords Donoughmore, Meath, Wolseley, and Ardilaun were prominent officials of the Immigration Reform Association. See *Times*, 22 May 1903. For a discussion of immigration restriction activities in America see J. Higham, *op. cit.*, pp. 35-105, 158-93, and B. M. Solomon, *op. cit.*, pp. 82 ff. In his presidential address to the Anthropological section of the British Association in August 1904, Arthur Balfour tried to belittle arguments that the English race was deteriorating, but he did admit that the younger generations in the cities were growing smaller and darker, and that the older Teutonic or "Germanic characteristics" in the people were giving way to more Southern racial types. *Spectator*, 27 August 1904, p. 277.

24. Dicey to Bryce, 17 May 1912, Bryce MS 3, ff. 113-16.

25. A. J. Balfour, "A Note on Home Rule," in S. Rosenbaum, ed., *Against Home Rule* (London, 1912), pp. 42-44.

26. See Bryce's revealing Creighton Lecture, "Race Sentiment as a Factor in History" (London, 1915), p. 5. The reception of Chamberlain's book in England, after it had sold over 60,000 copies in Germany, would make an interesting story. Lord Redesdale, in his introduction to the English edition, described the work as a "simple delight . . . fulfilling the highest function of which a teacher is capable, that of awakening thought and driving it into new channels. That is the charm of this book." p. viii. For Chamberlain's discussion of the racial ties between Celts and Teutons and their membership in the great Germanic race, see *The Foundations of the Nineteenth Century* (London, 1912), I, pp. 498-505, 511 ff.

Chapter IX

1. "To the Rose upon the Rood of Time" from *The Collected Poems of W. B. Yeats* (New York, 1966), p. 31.

2. The 'Milesian origins thesis' in Irish historiography and mythology is an old one, antedating Keating's account of the origins of the early inhabitants of Ireland. Its acceptance was implicit in Carlyle's reference to "the wild Milesian features" of Irishmen; and, presumably, it survives the latest reprint of Seumas MacManus, *The Story of the Irish Race* (New York, 1967), Chapter III, "The Milesians."

3. As O'Nolan exclaimed in Joyce's *Ulysses* (Modern Library edition, New York, 1942), p. 319.

4. A few examples out of a long list: the Ossianic Society, the Society for the Preservation of the Irish Language, the Ancient Order of Hibernians, the Gaelic Society, the Gaelic Athletic Association, the Philo-Celtic Society of New York and Boston, the Pan-Celtic Society, and, of course, the Gaelic League. A number of these organizations had branches in all the major cities of Greater Ireland.

5. George Moore, *Hail and Farewell, Ave* (London, 1925), I, p. 38. For another contrived version of that 'beginning' see Holbrook Jackson, *The Eighteen Nineties* (London, 1913), Chapter X, "The Discovery of the Celt," pp. 178-89.

6. There are many works worth consulting on the Celtic revival of the late nineteenth century, from W. P. Ryan, *The Irish Literary Revival* (London, 1894) to W. I. Thompson, *The Imagination of an Insurrection* (New York, 1967), but none of them penetrates to the ethnocentric substrata of that movement.

7. Geoffrey Keating, *The History of Ireland*, eds., David Comyn and P. S. Dinneen (London, 1902-14) 4 vols., published for the Irish Texts Society.

8. See Edward D. Snyder, *The Celtic Revival in English Literature, 1760-1800* (Cambridge, Mass., 1923).

9. The precursor of the RSAI was the Kilkenny Archaeological Society founded in 1849, which became the Royal Historical and Archaeological Society in 1869, before undergoing the second reincarnation of 1890.

10. The first director of the *Revue Celtique* was H. Gaidoz. This important journal was intended to improve the communication among Celticists around the world, and to a large extent it succeeded in this aim. Another German scholar of note was Heinrich Zimmer, author of *The Irish*

Element in Mediaeval Culture (New York, 1891) and *Keltische Studien* (Berlin, 1884). Kuno Meyer and Whitley Stokes founded the *Archiv für Celtische Lexikographie* in 1897.

11. See Denis Gwynn, *Young Ireland and 1848* (Cork, 1949), pp. 1-58; T. W. Moody, "Thomas Davis and the Irish Nation," *Hermathena*, No. 103 (Autumn, 1966), pp. 5-31; Sir C. Gavan Duffy, *My Life in Two Hemispheres* (New York, 1898), I, pp. 42-194, and *Young Ireland* (New York, 1881), pp. 151-65.

12. "Celts and Saxons," in *The Poems of Thomas Davis*, intro. by John Mitchel (New York, 1879), pp. 53-56.

13. To cite a few out of many examples of the surge in folklore publications: Lady Wilde, *Ancient Legends, Mystic Charms, and Superstitions of Ireland* (London, 1888), Patrick Kennedy, *Legendary Fictions of the Irish Celts* (London, 1891), Joseph Jacobs, *Celtic Fairy Tales* (London, 1892), Standish O'Grady, *The Bog of Stars* (Dublin, 1893) and *The Coming of Cuculain* (Dublin, 1894).

14. For a discussion of the ideas and careers of D. P. Moran and W. P. Ryan see Brian Inglis, "Moran of the *Leader* and Ryan of the *Irish Peasant*" in C. C. O'Brien, ed., *The Shaping of Modern Ireland* (London, 1960), pp. 108-23.

15. D. Hyde, "The Necessity for De-Anglicising Ireland," in G. Sigerson, ed., *The Revival of Irish Literature* (Dublin, 1894), pp. 117-61.

16. Take the case of Lady Gregory. Although Douglas Hyde expressed his pleasure over her translations of his "Irish pieces" in 1900, he found it necessary to correct her Irish spelling and vocabulary two years later. See Hyde to Lady Gregory, 5 June 1900 and 14 March 1902, Gregory MS, Berg Collection, New York Public Library.

17. Hyde's own quandary about the ethnocentrism of the Gaelic League emerges from a letter he wrote to Lady Gregory on 7 Jan. 1901: "The fact is that we cannot turn our back on the Davis ideal of every person in Ireland being an Irishman, no matter what their blood and politics, for the moment we cease to profess that, we land ourselves in an intolerable position. It is equally true, though, that the Gaelic League and the *Leader* aim at stimulating the old peasant, Papist aboriginal population, and we care very little about the others, though I would not let this be seen as Moran has done." Gregory MS, Berg Collection, N.Y. Public Library. The political implications of Hyde's Celticism may be seen to effect in his essay "The Return of the Fenians," in Lady Gregory, ed., *Ideals in Ireland* (London, 1901), pp. 65-67.

18. A. S. Green, *Irish Nationality* (London, 1911), p. 28. See also *The Making of Ireland and Its Undoing, 1200-1600* (London, 1908).

19. See Sophie Bryant, *Liberty, Order and Law Under Native Irish Rule* (London, 1923) and A. S. Green, *The Old Irish World* (Dublin, 1912).

20. John O'Hart, *Irish Pedigrees: or The Origin and Stem of the Irish Nation* (Dublin, 1887) 2 vols. O'Hart was indebted to Keating's genealogical data in *The History of Ireland* (London, 1902-14), I, pp. 91-93, IV, pp. 11-118.

21. Edward O'Meagher Condon, *The Irish Race in America* (Glasgow, n.d.), Chapter I. Condon used the phrase 'Greater Ireland' which appeared on the cover of his book, published around 1887.

22. Lord Castletown's presidential address to the second meeting of the Pan-Celtic Congress, held at Carnarvon, Wales, in the summer of 1904, contained some lyrical passages about the intuitive powers of the Celt. *North Wales Observer and Express*, 2 Sept. 1904.

23. For examples of American-Irish Celticism see Carl Wittke, *op. cit.*, pp. 161-71, and Handlin, *op. cit.*, pp. 140-55 ff., and above all, C. J. Herlihy, *The Celt Above the Saxon* (Boston, 1904).

24. For a striking example of this 'racyness' see Seumas MacManus, *The Story of the Irish Race*, which was first published in 1921, since when it has run through numerous editions and reprintings. MacManus wrote of Sinn Fein's rise: "The centre of gravity in national life changed from the anglicised towns to the rural population, sturdy, unspoilt, patriotic, virile, the offspring and living representatives of the traditional Gael. Hence, Irish politics began forthwith to reflect the mind of the real Irish race." p. 685. An apotheosis of 'the Irish mind' that surpasses all others for sheer fantasy is Sophie Bryant's, *The Genius of the Gael* (London, 1913).

25. See Pearse's famous speech of 31 March 1912 in Dublin in which, speaking in Irish, he threatened "red war in Ireland" if the Gall tried to trick the Gael over Home Rule. Quoted in Dorothy Macardle, *The Irish Republic* (New York, 1965), p. 82.

Chapter X

1. See Elie Halévy's treatment of Pan-Teutonism in *A History of the English People in the Nineteenth Century*, V, *Imperialism and the Rise of Labour* (London, 1951), pp. 41-68.

2. Earnest A. Hooton and C. W. Dupertuis, *The Physical Anthropology of Ireland* in *Papers of the Peabody Museum of Archaeology and Ethnology*, Harvard University, Vol. XXX, Nos. 1-2 (Cambridge, Mass., 1955).

The authors of this remarkable study arrived at an ethnological typology for the Irish people made up of the following divisions: Pure Nordic, Predominantly Nordic, Keltic, East Baltic, Dinaric, Nordic Mediterranean, Pure Mediterranean, and Nordic Alpine. The photographs provided in part II give some indication of the variety of facial features and head shapes observed by these two investigators.

3. "My patriotism knows no geographical but only racial limits. I am an Imperialist and not a Little Englander, because I am a British Race Patriot. . . . This brings us to our first great principle — follow the race. . . . We cannot afford to part with so much of our best blood. . . ." Quoted in A. M. Gollin, *Proconsul in Politics* (London, 1964), pp. 128-29.

4. The quality of "magic" by means of which the imperial Prospero held the colonial Caliban in his grasp is discussed in both O. Mannoni, *Prospero and Caliban* (New York, 1964, 2nd edn.), and P. Mason, *Prospero's Magic* (London, 1962). Christopher Fyfe has recently written that "race was perhaps the strongest supporting mechanism of the British Empire"; and the evidence collected for this study would support his position and invalidate A. P. Thornton's bald assertion in *The Imperial Idea and Its Enemies* (London, 1959) that "British patriotism has never been racial." See *Race*, VIII (Oct., 1966), p. 195.

5. G. M. Young, *op. cit.*, p. 186.

6. Sir William Orpen, the artist, has some amusing lines about the ways in which Irish jarvey and cab drivers used to play up to their wealthy English fares or clients by acting the role of Paddy. The reward for Paddy stories was usually a handsome tip. See *Stories of Old Ireland and Myself* (London, 1924), pp. 75-76.

7. The similarity between the stereotypical traits assigned by Anglo-Saxonists to Irishmen and by some white Americans to Negroes is more than coincidental. Kimball Young provides one set of 'racial traits' for the Negro in his *An Introductory Sociology* (New York, 1934), pp. 158-63, which, except for such categories as "primitive morality" and gaudy dress, bears a strong resemblance to Paddy in every respect, from emotional instability to indolence and violence. Quoted in G. Allport, *op. cit.*, pp. 192-93.

Select Bibliography

Listed below are some of the books and articles which have proved most useful in preparing this essay. For reasons of space I have omitted from the list all the major works of the Anglo-Saxonist historians, from Sharon Turner, Kemble, Kingsley, Green, Freeman, and Stubbs to Froude, Smith, and Lecky. Other relevant works are cited in the notes.

T. W. Adorno *et al.*, *The Authoritarian Personality* (New York, 1964), 2 vols. Contains controversial and suggestive approaches to the study of ethnic and racial prejudices.

Gordon W. Allport, *The Nature of Prejudice* (Cambridge, Mass., 1954). A comprehensive and lucid introduction to the subject.

Charles M. Andrews, *The Old English Manor* (Baltimore, 1892). Provides an important critique of the mark theory.

Matthew Arnold, *On the Study of Celtic Literature and Other Essays* (London, n.d.), Everyman edn. A classic expression of ethnological superstitions and Celticist archetypes.

W. J. Ashley, *Surveys Historic and Economic* (New York, 1900). Contains a useful summary of the controversy over the mark theory.

W. D. Babington, *Fallacies of Race Theories as Applied to National Characteristics* (London, 1895). A significant attack on race thinking by an environmentalist.

J. O. Bartley, *Teague, Shenkin and Sawney* (Cork, 1954). An excellent guide to the portrayal of Irish, Welsh, and Scottish stereotypes on the English stage before 1800.

Jacques Barzun, *Race, A Study in Superstition* (New York, 1965). A new edition of an older standard introduction to race thinking in general and Celticism in particular.

John Beddoe, *The Races of Britain* (Bristol & London, 1885). A fascinating example of later Victorian physical ethnology and anthropology.

Bruno Bettelheim and M. Janowitz, *The Dynamics of Prejudice* (New York, 1950). Important for the study of intolerant personalities.

M. D. Biddiss, "Gobineau and the Origins of European Racism," *Race*, VII (Jan., 1966), pp. 255-70. A cogent discussion of Gobineau's theories on race.

Stephen J. Brown, *Ireland in Fiction* (Dublin, 1919). An invaluable bibliography for students of Paddy in novels.

Sophie Bryant, *The Genius of the Gael* (London, 1913). A classic example of Celticist thinking about the psychic qualities of Irishmen.

James Bryce, *The Relations of the Advanced and Backward Races of Mankind* (Oxford, 1902); *Race Sentiment as a Factor in History* (London, 1915). Two lectures revealing the ambivalence of a prominent Liberal on the subject of race.

J. W. Burrow, *Evolution and Society, A Study in Victorian Social Theory* (Cambridge, Eng., 1966). An illuminating but not definitive essay on evolutionary thought in Victorian England.

Peter T. Cominos, "Late Victorian Sexual Respectability and the Social System," *International Review of Social History*, VIII (1963), Parts I and II. A sociological interpretation of Victorian respectability and continence that deserves to be called seminal.

Edward O'M. Condon, *The Irish Race in America* (Glasgow, n.d.). A good example of Celticist myths designed for Greater Ireland.

Philip D. Curtin, *The Image of Africa* (Madison, 1964). A stimulating discussion of English images of West Africa from the 1780's through the 1840's.

Albert V. Dicey, *England's Case Against Home Rule* (London, 1886). A closely argued statement of the Unionist case, relatively free from overt Anglo-Saxonism.

Charles Dilke, *Greater Britain* (London, 1869). One of the finest examples of Anglo-Saxonist attitudes about the British Empire — old and new — and the importance of Anglo-Saxondom.

Sir Charles Gavan Duffy, *Young Ireland, A Fragment of Irish History* (New York, 1881). Reveals the ambiguous position of Young Ireland on the question of Irish race and nationality.

Waldo H. Dunn, *James Anthony Froude, A Biography* (Oxford, 1961, 1963), 2 vols. Useful for details of Froude's Irish experience.

Loren Eiseley, *Darwin's Century* (New York, 1958). An excellent introduction to English theories about evolution and heredity.

F. E. Faverty, *Matthew Arnold, The Ethnologist* (Evanston, 1951). Connects Arnold's essay on Celtic literature with then current ethnological beliefs.

J. A. Froude, *The Two Chiefs of Dunboy* (London, 1889). Fascinating story set in the west of Ireland, revealing Froude's profound prejudices.

J. Arthur de Gobineau, *The Inequality of Human Races* (London, 1915), trans. by A. Collins. Overrated and underread.

G. P. Gooch, *History and Historians in the Nineteenth Century* (Boston, 1959). A revision of the 1913 edition, valuable as a bibliographical guide; not interpretive.

Thomas F. Gosset, *Race, the History of an Idea in America* (Dallas, 1963). The best single introduction to Anglo-American race thinking in the nineteenth century.

Alice S. Green, *Irish Nationality* (London, 1911). Like most of her writings on Irish subjects, full of romantic Celticism.

Oscar Handlin, *Boston's Immigrants, 1790-1865; A Study in Acculturation* (Cambridge, Mass., 1941). Revised, enlarged, and brought up to 1880 in the 1959 edition, this work exposes many facets of Irish immigrant life in Boston.

John Higham, *Strangers in the Land, Patterns of American Nativism, 1860-1925* (New York, 1963). Invaluable for nativist attitudes toward Irish and European immigrants.

Christopher Hill, "The Norman Yoke," *Puritanism and Revolution* (London, 1962). A perceptive essay on the political significance of the Norman Conquest mythology since the seventeenth century.

Margaret T. Hodgen, *Early Anthropology in the Sixteenth and Seventeenth Centuries* (Philadelphia, 1964). An excellent work, especially useful for English theories about savages.

Earnest A. Hooton and C. W. Dupertuis, *The Physical Anthropology of Ireland* (Cambridge, Mass., 1955). Indispensable for those who wish to know the anthropological makeup of the Irish people.

Douglas Hyde, "The Necessity of De-Anglicising Ireland," *The Revival of Irish Literature* (London, 1894). Essential reading for any student of Irish Celticism.

Douglas Hyde, *A Literary History of Ireland* (New York, 1899). Chapter I discusses the origins of the Celts; important for twentieth century Celticists.

John A. Jackson, *The Irish in Britain* (London, 1963). Useful, descriptive introduction to an historical problem in need of further sociological investigation.

Geoffrey Keating, *The History of Ireland* (London, 1902-14). A classic work, elegant and perceptive, one of the first informed replies to English detractors of the Irish.

John V. Kelleher, "Matthew Arnold and the Celtic Revival," in Harry Levin, ed., *Perceptives of Criticism* (Cambridge, Mass., 1950). An acute and informed treatment of the literary dimensions of Arnold's essay.

Charles Kingsley, *The Roman and the Teuton* (London, 1875). Full of Anglo-Saxonist fantasies about European history.

Samuel Kliger, *The Goths in England* (Cambridge, Mass., 1952). Despite an awkward style a useful survey of Gothicist thought in the late 17th and 18th centuries.

Robert Knox, *The Races of Men* (London, 1850). Loaded with Anglo-Saxonist dogma about the importance of racial purity.

Elisabeth Lecky, *A Memoir of the Rt. Hon. W. E. H. Lecky* (New York, 1910, 2nd edn.). An articulate account of Lecky's career by his wife.

Godfrey Lienhardt, *Social Anthropology* (London, 1964). Chapter I contains a brief historical introduction to the subject.

Seumas MacManus, *The Story of the Irish Race* (New York, 1967). A popular piece of Celticist history first published in 1922.

Nicholas Mansergh, *The Irish Question, 1840-1921* (London, 1965). A revised version of the standard account of Anglo-Irish relations as seen by contemporaries. Conventional in its interpretation, but an important contribution

Philip Mason, ed., *Man, Race and Darwin* (London, 1960). Instructive symposium on varieties of race consciousness and prejudice.

Philip Mason, *Prospero's Magic* (London, 1962). A suggestive discussion of the interaction of race and class prejudice in the British imperial context.

O. Mannoni, *Prospero and Caliban, The Psychology of Colonization* (New York, 1956). A pioneering, personal, and therefore controversial appraisal of the French colonial experience in Madagascar.

Ashley Montagu, *Man's Most Dangerous Myth: The Fallacy of Race* (Cleveland, 1964). A stimulating study of race thinking, especially useful for 19th century European attitudes.

Henry Morley, ed., *Ireland Under Elizabeth and James I* (London, 1890). Contains some gruesome descriptions of Ireland by Davies, Moryson, and Spenser.

John Munro, *The Story of the British Race* (New York, 1907). An example of 'revisionist' Anglo-Saxonist ethnology.

Gunnar Myrdal, *An American Dilemma* (New York, 1957). This classic study of the Negro question in America implicitly invites comparisons with the Irish question in Britain.

C. C. O'Brien, ed., *The Shaping of Modern Ireland* (London, 1960). Chapters on D. P. Moran, W. P. Ryan and Gaelic Athletic Association useful for students of Celticism.

P. S. O'Hegarty, *A History of Ireland Under the Union, 1801 to 1922* (London, 1952). A non-academic survey of Irish political history full of quotations from Celticist spokesmen.

T. K. Penniman, *A Hundred Years of Anthropology* (London, 1935). Discusses the founding and personnel of London Ethnological and Anthropological Societies.

James Cowles Prichard, *The Eastern Origin of the Celtic Nations* (London, 1857). Illuminates the vital connection between philology and ethnology in the early Victorian period.

David B. Quinn, *The Elizabethans and the Irish* (Ithaca, 1966). A succinct account of English images of the Irish in Tudor times.

Ernest Renan, *The Poetry of the Celtic Races* (London, 1896), trans. by W. G. Hutchison. This essay inspired Arnold to inspire others with Celticist mythology.

A. A. Roback, *A Dictionary of International Slurs* (Cambridge, Mass., 1944). An unusual collection of ethnic terms, slurs, and jokes, for students of stereotypical thinking.

John M. Robertson, *The Saxon and the Celt, A Study in Sociology* (London, 1897). An incisive and perceptive attack on racialist myths in England.

Goldwin Smith, *Irish History and Irish Character* (Oxford, 1861). A polemical account of the Irish question written by a pronounced Anglo-Saxonist with radical pretensions.

Edward D. Snyder, "The Wild Irish: A Study of Some English Satires against the Irish, Scots, and Welsh," *Modern Philology*, XVII (April, 1920), pp. 147-85. Useful compilation of pre-nineteenth-century stereotypes of the Irish and other 'Celts.'

Barbara M. Solomon, *Ancestors and Immigrants* (Cambridge, Mass., 1956). Valuable study of ethnocentrism in New England during second half of nineteenth century.

William Stanton, *The Leopard's Spots, Scientific Attitudes Toward Race in America, 1815-59* (Chicago, 1966). A stimulating account of early American ethnology and anthropology.

W. R. W. Stephens, *The Life and Letters of Edward A. Freeman* (London, 1895) 2 vols. Indispensable for students of Freeman and Anglo-Saxonist historiography.

Carl Wittke, *The Irish in America* (Baton Rouge, 1956). A useful survey based on extensive newspaper sources.

Note on Manuscript Sources

Among the manuscript collections consulted in the course of composing this essay were the papers of James, Viscount Bryce and Sir Matthew Nathan in the Bodleian Library, Oxford; the papers of Joseph Chamberlain in the University of Birmingham Library, Birmingham; the papers of Lady Gregory in the Berg Collection, New York Public Library; and the papers of Sir Horace Plunkett at Plunkett House, London. For access to these collections and for permission to publish extracts from them, I am indebted to the curators, keepers, and trustees, as the case may be.

INDEX

STUDIES IN BRITISH HISTORY AND CULTURE